The Masters Guide to Cunnilingus

How to Perform Successful Oral Sex and Provide the Highest Degree of Pleasure Possible

Vanessa Ryan

Outskirts Press, Inc.
Denver, Colorado

The opinions expressed in this manuscript are solely the opinions of the author and do not represent the opinions or thoughts of the publisher. The author represents and warrants that s/he either owns or has the legal right to publish all material in this book. If you believe this to be incorrect, contact the publisher through its website at www.outskirtspress.com.

The Masters Guide to Cunnilingus
How to Perform Successful Oral Sex and Provide the Highest Degree of Pleasure Possible
All Rights Reserved
Copyright © 2006 Vanessa Ryan

This book may not be reproduced, transmitted, or stored in whole or in part by any means, including graphic, electronic, or mechanical without the express written consent of the publisher except in the case of brief quotations embodied in critical articles and reviews.

Outskirts Press
http://www.outskirtspress.com

ISBN-10: 1-59800-609-6
ISBN-13: 978-1-59800-609-4

Outskirts Press and the "OP" logo are trademarks belonging to Outskirts Press, Inc.

Printed in the United States of America

Table of Contents

*Setting the Mood with Sensual Foreplay, Erotic

Massage, Talking, Kissing, Fantasy   1

*Aphrodisiacs: Arousing Desire   14

*The Anatomy of Female Sexual Arousal   17

*The G-Spot, the A-Spot & the Clit:

An Orgasmic Combo   23

*Taste & Smell of the "Love Flowers"   33

*Cunnilingus Licking & Eating Pussy: Getting Started 36

*Essential Tongue Techniques & Exercises	45
*Golden Fingers: The Double Pleasure Clamp Rules	52
*Advanced Oral Sex Stimulation	54
*Cunnilingus Positions to Make Her Squirt	57
*Innovate Oral Sex Positions	59
*Ten Worst Cunnilingus Mistakes	65
*Tips to Please Her & Cunnilingus Curious Facts	68
*Kamasutra after Oral Sex	75
*Fantasies and Practices	103
*Vibrators, Dildos and Lubricants	109
*Safe Oral Sex & Sexually Transmitted Diseases	113

Setting the Mood with Sensual Foreplay, Erotic Massage, Talking, Kissing, Fantasy

Ahhh, "cunnilingus."
This is the way most women react when asked how they feel about receiving oral sex.

Men need direction too - Cunnilingus is one of the most difficult sexual acts to perform successfully. Going down isn't easy. It takes refined skill combined with patience, healthy free-flowing communication with one's partner and energy for the long haul. Cunnilingus, "muff diving," "eating pussy" or whatever you want to call it is one of the most beautiful and intimate activities to grace this planet.

Compared to penetrative sex, oral sex performed on a woman results in a greater likelihood of orgasm, if done correctly. Many women prefer it to intercourse because they find it the easiest way to come aside from masturbation.

What makes it so great? It definitely has something to do with the clit being the sole source of 80% of all women's orgasms. Women love oral sex. There are many reasons why.

First, nothing else feels as good as a warm, wet tongue sliding across a woman's vulva and clitoris. Second, it is a powerful show of love and intimacy and suggests how much you love your partner and want her to achieve sexual fulfillment. Third, it offers profound intimacy and allows women to rapidly lose themselves into sheer sexual pleasure. And fourth, no matter what the size of your penis, you can give good head. Truly, a man with good cunnilingus skills can be the most popular lover in the world! When a woman finds a man who gives good head, she's found a treasure she's not going to let go of too quickly. Moreover, when a good session of cunnilingus, which in itself is almost guaranteed to bring a woman off, is combined with your finger stimulating her G-spot, the blend of clitoral and G-spot stimulation produces an orgasm far more intense and fulfilling than clitoral stimulation alone. This is rather convenient, because with your head down there, you are in just the right place to provide the added excitement of G-spot stimulation. Most guys can fuck, and those who can usually do it satisfactorily, but the guy who gives good head, he's got it made it!

The reason why women love oral sex is basically the same as the reason why men love oral sex - women love to be truly loved by a man rather than used or abused as housemaids, cooks or simple friend instead of true partner for life. To be loved is nothing to explain - nor something to intellectually learn or even to pretend or fake - to be truly loved always requires to be fully accepted as a sexual being. There are but a few ways to ultimately and beyond any doubt prove to accept a woman as a female partner for life - one of the most powerful is true oral love - or oral sex - leading to a fast, relaxing and healing orgasm in the female partner. What woman does not love to be expertly eaten out? Oral sex done right can take your partner to new heights of pleasure, but done wrong it can be an ordeal for both of you.

Eating pussy can be one of the most wonderful things you can do for a woman. It makes her feel appreciated, respected, desirable, and has the potential to give her an orgasm that will

The Masters Guide to Cunnilingus

shatter glass, raise the dead, and even wake you in the next room. Besides, lots of women expect it these days, and men who perform great oral sex are always in demand. If you gain a reputation as an expert, many classy, attractive women, way out of your league, may overlook your other shortcomings.

Love making is an experience where you are with your partner and experience the ultimate pleasure and it definitely helps fight tension and stress. To achieve maximum pleasure and to arouse to the peak level, both the partners need extra spice, and that is attained in foreplay. Love making is considered as one of the most efficient way to get close to your partner; you are with your soul-mate and have prepared yourself to forget all other things and set your mind to attain the ultimate experience, foreplay allows you do exactly the same. It is not only restricted to bodily pleasure, but it's a moment when both the partners dedicate themselves to each other.

Foreplay is a fundamental part of the whole lovemaking experience. It is important for the learning experience. Foreplay is the perfect time to spend time understanding what your partner likes because without that, you will never understand what they really need to be fully stimulated. Foreplay helps your partner get involved herself completely and allow you make her feel special. One good reason to why foreplay needed is that men can move from one mood to another very easily for example if a person is watching match he can be ready at very next moment to have sex but women take more time to arouse and get into mood, they are more aware of setting, surrounding and mood. They need to be romanced to make them get involved 100%. Today, foreplay has become an integral part of the whole lovemaking experience. It is true that impromptu sexual encounters without foreplay can sometimes be some of the best sexual experiences, but in general, most women will agree that good sexual encounters should include long and sensual foreplay. A more vigilant form of foreplay will bring increased pleasures to both partners, and make the lovemaking experience more enjoyable. The man will need to prolong foreplay to get an erection and the women will need the same to become properly lubricated. Most sex experts agree that there is no such thing as spending too much time on foreplay. First of all, men who cuddle and kiss their partners and know how to enjoy sensitive foreplay will often find that their partners will reach orgasm more often!

Generally guys tend to want to skip over foreplay to get straight to sex. Sometimes a quickie can be great, but generally, the more time you spend fore playing, teasing, and not touching any genital area, the more fantastic the sex will be. The whole idea of foreplay is to take your time. One of the things that people often complain about is that foreplay takes too much time. Some people may say that sex should be spontaneous, but if sex never happens or is always hurried, then where is the fun in that? There is also the element of having something to look forward to, and that in and of itself can be erotic and a form of foreplay.

Verbal Foreplay

An interesting little idea is for one partner to control the foreplay verbally. One partner is the talker, one is the doer. Remember that women are more verbal than men so when it comes to sex or foreplay, talking can be an important part of the experience, and can result in more sex pleasure for both of you. Talking is a very important aspect of foreplay. If the purpose of foreplay is to get both lovers ready, more excited, ramped up for orgasm, then talking sexy is one of the best ways. If you and your lover do not talk sexy to each other you do not know what you are missing. When was the last time you called her up in the middle of the day to tell her that you can't wait to get home and lick her muffin? Well, start doing it. Her anticipation alone will make your touch feel that much more exaggerated. Start seducing her without having to make love to her all the time. Anticipation can be one of the greatest aphrodisiacs. Grab her and give her a deep kiss for no reason. Talk about what you plan to do to her sexually when you take her out for dinner. These little things will keep her mind working when you are finally penetrating. A whisper in a naughty place can be very exciting. The party with friends' night can be enhanced by whispering sweet and sexy things to your lover. Say something like "you are sexier then any woman here tonight" and watch your lovers response. During sex talk dirty. This can be the basis of a steamy sexual encounter especially if your lover is not expecting it. Just start to talk like a gigolo. Talk about your lover as if she is the only sexual being worthy of your time and especially talk about how she make you feel. Tell her how SEXY she is and how sweet she tastes! Women love to be touched, and felt. She wants to feel your hands on her body. It is a very important physical connection that sends messages to her most intimate senses. When a man touches a woman's body, she feels wanted, she feels lusted, she feels craved, but most of all she feels SEXY! You want her to feel SEXY!

Let her know how good she feels to you. Let her know that she is driving you crazy. Women also love to know that for sure. When men are quiet during sex, women feel that they are not exciting or sexy. Women need to hear that men want them and want to please them. Use sweet words and make her feel special and you might be surprised how much this will add to the passion!

Erotic Massage

Erotic massage is really a sexual foreplay technique, rather than a form of massage. Massage focuses on muscles, whereas erotic massage focuses primarily on skin. It's been said that 95% of erotic (or sensual) massage is the same as other massage. Everyone likes to be touched in that sensual kind of way. And although we all love massages, they are always a thousand times more enjoyable when done by a sexy lover. Massages can be used for anything from calming your lover down from a tough day at work to getting her primed for some enthusiastic lovemaking. Touch is very important. It does not always mean that the person who is touching wants sex. Humans need that caring physical contact, on a daily basis. That is what is so wonderful about massage. It allows us to experience that sensual world of touch without pressures of having sex. Of course, there is nothing wrong with ending a massage with sex, but what is important is it does not have to end that way. Massage is wonderful way to get close and sensual with someone you care deeply about. Massage is inherently sexual, and you can make it more or less sexual depending on how each of you feels when you are giving the massage. Unless you so relax her that she is more asleep than awake, there is a good chance your efforts will arouse her because of the intimacy, and because the massage will release a great deal of oxytocin into her body. If she is open to it, massage can be a great form of foreplay, first relaxing her, and then arousing her. If you get it just right, you will not be allowed to finish the massage! Close the lights and ignite lots of scented candles and create a relaxing environment. Aromatherapy can be a big payoff but select something that is lightly scented and neutral. Turn on some sexy, relaxing music, and most importantly turn off the ringer on your phone.

Feet

To start, have her take a bath or shower. To make it even nicer give her a bubble bath (prepare it for her and help her wash) or get in the shower with her and do the washing for her. Have a small pillow for her head, and another to put under her legs just above the feet - a hand towel over the pillows will protect them from the massage oil. Use good massage oil, and apply the oil to your hands, not directly to her skin. Start at her feet, and work up, slowly! Now here is a very sensitive area of the body. Massaging the feet can sometimes be massaging the soul. Some people can be very ticklish, so it might do you good before find out before head, so your lover does not start flailing about when you accidentally tickle her. If your lover has very ticklish feet make sure you use a firmer grip and apply more pressure. Most of the time, a lighter touch is what drives people crazy. If she is super sensitive, then you might want to avoid the feet altogether. Grab her foot, soles of feet facing you with thumbs on soles and finger on top of feet. Move your thumbs in a circular motion while applying pressure to the balls of the feet.

Then massage each toe by lightly squeezing it between your thumb and index finger, then gently pulling on each one.

Neck and Shoulders

The shoulders and neck are common tension spots. The sooner you start to work out those knots the more relaxing your partner will be for the rest of the massage, resulting in more enjoyment. Apply a dime-size drop of oil into your palms and rub your hands together to make sure your hands are warm, then fan your hands out on her upper back and align your thumbs about an inch away from each other on either side of the spinal cord. Using tips of your fingers and thumb, not your nails, gently grip your partner's shoulders and knead the skin. But make sure you grab a good amount of skin as to not pinch. And do not do it hard and fast. The key is slow end gentle. If you do not use gentle pressure, your partner will tense up and by pulling and pushing against a tense muscle, you could bruise it. So take it easy. Another good technique on the neck is to place one hand on either side of the neck and apply a small amount of pressure. Then move your hands in a circular motion. Remember slow and gentle circles. As you're doing this, work your hands up behind your partner's ears and back down to the shoulders.

Back, Sides and Buttocks

At this point you can work your way down your partner's back. Now the back is the center of any massage because it is composed of three large groups of muscles. Continue this circular motion with both hands on each side of the spine. And spread out your hands and the area you cover to include the sides and lower back too. Now try some light feathery touches all over the back, side and lower back. Use both hands, one on each side of the spine and rub in a diagonal motion from the spine out. Use small, quick strokes. After that lightly rub your hands all over your partner's back. One key to a good massage is after you do anything that may be a little on the rougher side, do something light, smooth and soft to connect all those areas you just worked on. Now you are ready to tackle the buttocks. Using the inside of your forearm, slowly rub one butt cheek at a time in large circular motions. When finished with that, make a fist and roll your knuckles, one by one, over the triangular bone at her lower back. This is another area that holds an awful lot of stress. So take care when applying pressure.

Legs

Kneel at your lover's side, oil up your hands and grab her ankle and knead with your thumbs and fingers all the way up her leg. Do not use too much pressure behind the knees because it could injure sensitive veins. Once you reach the thighs, rub your entire hands in a circular motion and knead the skin. Just be careful, the thighs can be highly erogenous zones, so if you want to finish your massage, make sure you take care.

Head and Face

The best way to end a massage is by massaging your lover's head and face. This brings it full circle and also brings you closer to your lover, allowing the two of you to be intimate with each other. A head massage can be wonderfully relaxing and arousing. Of course, to massage the head, you do not need any massage oil. You might actually want to have a towel handy so you can wipe your hands off before the head massage. Start by gently stroking your fingers through her hair. If her hair is long make sure you do not get your fingers stuck in knots, so be careful. Using the tips of your fingers, gently knead her head, the whole head. Work your way over the temples and use the tips of your first two or three fingers. Gently rub in a circular motion. Then lightly run your fingers across her entire face. Using your finger tips lightly tap her face, like raindrops were falling from the sky. With your thumb and first finger, rub your lover's earlobes and ears. Then lightly run your hands over her eyes, eyebrows, and lastly lips. If you want to get more intimate, gently kiss your lover on the eyelids, tip of nose and lips.

Kissing

Many people find kissing to be the fundamental act of foreplay. Kissing involves a range of behaviors from very light lip-to-lip contact, to what is often referred to as "deep" or French kissing, in which partners rub their tongues against each other and over other mouth surfaces. Generally, kissing is considered to be an extremely intimate and pleasurable act because it involves direct face-to-face contact and because the mucous membranes that cover the lips and mouth have an especially dense supply of nerve endings. Some individuals are particularly sensitive around their ears, inner thighs, or lower stomach, while breasts and nipples often are highly preferred places for caressing and oral stimulation. There is much more to a kiss than just lips and tongues. To experience the full pleasure of the act you have to be resourceful! Do not forget to use your hands, your nose, and even your breath to elevate your passionate kissing ventures to a new level. Women love to be touched while she is being kissed. Use your hands to gently caress her cheek, her back, the tops of her arms, and especially her collarbone and jawbone right before and during the kiss. Rubbing noses is also extremely pleasurable, and can cause some sexual giggles between the two of you. Giggles are always a sure sign that you are making them feel special. Using your breath is also important. Providing your partner with extremely light, warm feelings on their face, neck, and mouth can be an extremely arousing feeling. Most women complain that their partners do not kiss long enough and rush the movement directly to the genital area. Do not be shy to experiment on every part of her body and remember to prolong the foreplay with more kissing and caressing.

A good kiss can be a huge turn-on and a promise of greater things to come in the bedroom. A bad kiss on the other hand, can kill your chances in the sack before you get a foot in the front door. We'll tell you how to become an irresistible kisser with these simple pointers.

Start slow, and then turn up the heat

It may be tempting on the first kiss to go full throttle and try to express all your pent-up passion in a melting lip-lock, but overly eager kissing from the get-go can scare your partner off. Really, it is far sexier to begin slowly and gently and build to a fiery crescendo. Think of it like starting a fire; first you need a spark and some kindling. Depending on your moods, it may take only a few seconds of smooching for the flames to ignite.

First lips, then tongue

Keep your lips relaxed and slightly parted as they contact your partner's. Don't immediately dart your tongue into her mouth. First let your tongue gently brush against her lips and wait for her to yield for more. If she responds by touching your tongue with hers, consider that an invitation to enter, Keep your tongue flexible and responsive; don't stiffen it to a point, but don't let it go completely flaccid either.

Leave breathing room

Make sure you don't block your partner's airways. Avoid getting in a position where your noses are shushed, and come up occasionally for air.

Also, don't forget to breathe while you're kissing; you can inhale and exhale discreetly through your nose even while joined at the lips.

Give and take

Kissing is like dancing with a partner; you have to be in the moment, sensitive and attentive to your partner's rhythm,

The Masters Guide to Cunnilingus

moves, and mood. The best kissing has a back and forth, call-and-response quality. Try something and see if she responds positively, either vocally or with her mouth. If she digs it, continue and elaborate, or follow her lead for a while.

Use just enough saliva

"Swapping spit" is just an expression. Moisten your tongue and lips with just enough saliva to keep things slippery and lubricated, so your lips slide easily against your partner's.

No one enjoys kisses that are either dry and chafing or sloppy and slobbery.

Nibble, gently

Gently using your teeth to nibble or tug on a partner's lip can be extremely sexy, but the key is to do it *gently.* The edges of your teeth can be sharp on the sensitive tissues of the lips and mouth. Take your partner's lower lip between your lips and gently suck it in between your open teeth. Then use your teeth to apply the slightest possible pressure on her lip. Don't nip! You don't want to draw blood.

Use your hands

Use your hands to touch your partner in ways that complement the kiss. Caress her face, her ears, the back of her neck, and her hair.

This is very romantic. Depending on your position, you may choose to do more, but don't use the kiss as a distraction so you can make a grab for her breasts or ass. Proceed slowly as you explore other areas.

Less can be more

Some of the sexiest moments in kissing come your lips are barely touching your partner's. Try it. Pull back for a second and take a moment to gaze in her eyes as you lightly brush your lips against hers. If done correctly, this can cause the world to stop for a pulse-pounding moment and she will swoon.

Stay focused

Many guys think of kissing as the prelude to heavier making out or sex.

It certainly can be, but while you're kissing, you have to stay focused on the moment. She will know if your mind is wandering or you're trying to figure out to how to get her bra undone. Think of the kiss as an end in itself, not an avenue to her underwear.

Use your mouth to seduce

Use your lips and your tongue to leave your lover wanting more. Your kissing should say, "This is just a taste of what I've got for you." Many women judge a guy's potential as a lover by the way he kisses: a sensitive, attentive, passionate kisser equals dynamite in the sack, while a sloppy, pushy kisser equals a dud. If you can demonstrate your prowess in mouth-to-mouth contact alone, she'll be leading you to the bedroom in no time.

Fantasy

Sexual fantasies are an intriguing subject...and not only men have them. The truth is, women have them too, but they are limited to three general types. Women can be just as sexual as a man if he learns what fantasy buttons to push.

In order to rouse a woman's fantasies, it takes a little work. First of all, when you set out to stimulate your partner, you need to narrow your focus down to the three specific types of fantasies: 1. Women with women, 2. Women in Control, and 3. Sexually insatiable.

Too often, when using fantasies, men include the things that turn themselves on rather than what arouses a woman.

Unfortunately, this is the quickest way to turn a woman off. Women have specific requirements in their fantasies, primarily, a slow building pace before and after the sex act. As a matter of fact, the non-sexual touching is equally arousing to a woman. When using fantasies with your partner, pay close attention to the core elements in each of the types listed below and include those details during fantasy talk.

Fantasy one: Women with Women. This fantasy is alluring to women because its primary activities consists of two aspects of sex that women crave: oral satisfaction and tenderness. The key to this fantasy is slow seduction. It begins with caressing and holding, builds to passionate, mutual orgasms, and finishes the way it began-tenderly.

Fantasy Two: Women in Control. The central theme in this fantasy is a woman who has the power to maker her partner cum. This is the woman who plays the controlling seductress whether it's through the role of dominatrix, exhibitionist, or any number of controlling women roles that turn a man on. Her arousal comes from watching a man lose his control to her.

Fantasy Three: Sexually Insatiable. Unlike the other two types of fantasies, this one is more "manly" because the focus is on the sex act. Common themes in these fantasies are: engaging in forbidden love, oral sex, multiple orgasms, orgies, public sex, and anything involving sexually adventurous actions.

The easiest way to begin is to start out slowly. You might, for instance, bring up the topic of sexual fantasies. All you need to say is, Which of the following three would turn you on more? At that time, mention the fantasies above. The mere act of talking about it will arouse her.

So, if you want to turn your partner on through sexual fantasies, all you have to do is start talking about the subject. It may be a slow process, but it's guaranteed to create an insatiable woman!

Aphrodisiacs: Arousing Desire

By definition, an aphrodisiac is a substance such as food, drink, drug or other that promotes sexual desire.

History and beliefs

Since time immemorial, many types of food have been considered aphrodisiacs.

In ancient Greece, temple priestesses were experts in the art of making love potions. Their fame was such that their sanctuaries attracted travellers from all corners of the Empire. All their recipes used garlic, "that renders women loving and men strong". Greek athletes also absorbed large amounts of fresh garlic to strengthen their muscles, even though they called it "stinking rose".

Romans believed nuts, dates and pistachios were aphrodisiacs, because they resembled testicles.

In the Middle Ages, people concocted all number of potions and elixirs designed to stimulate sexual desire. Eating the genitals of various animals was also considered an aphrodisiac.

Early colonisers of Africa even (falsely) believed that the rhinoceros horn had aphrodisiac properties.- Throughout history, foods whose shape, texture or smell are evocative of the male or female genitalia or sexual fluids have been seen as aphrodisiacs. Asparagus, celery, oysters, caviar, bananas, peeled tomatoes, carrots and ginger are often considered aphrodisiacs. Spices have also been included in this category as they elevate body temperature.

The effectiveness of aphrodisiacs

The effectiveness of aphrodisiacs is on the whole very relative and untrustworthy. Their effect is more psychological than physical. They seem to function only for those who believe in them. In reality, only some narcotic substances have proved aphrodisiac properties, but they present important health hazards. A good meal in an intimate locale and sensual atmosphere, with evocative foods, can arouse the desire for the couple to make love. Pleasant perfumes can play a role as well.

Two substances might have real aphrodisiac properties, but they are dangerous to your health :

-The Spanish Fly, for men. This substance is made of crushed coccinella (ladybirds). Rubbing the Spanish Fly against the urethra provokes an irritation that may generate sexual desire. But beware : this substance is very toxic! Actually, the flasks of "Spanish Fly" sold in specialized stores usually contain nothing but vitamin concentrates, and their effectiveness is far from proven.

-The yohimbine is an extract made from the bark of an African tree. Its effectiveness has allegedly been demonstrated, and it is believed to induce erections in men or sexual arousal in women, by dilating blood vessels in the genitals. However, absorbing yohimbine is risky because it can induce a dangerous drop in the blood pressure.

More ordinary pleasure-inducing substance

A few common items may induce a certain stimulation of the sexual desire :

Bitter Chocolate

Biological research conducted on pure chocolate concludes that its aromas stimulate the brain and have an effect on sexual arousal.

Wine and Champagne

In certain cultures or religions, wine was thought to have a divine origin and has been, or still is, considered an aphrodisiac. Casanova, the great Venetian seducer, gave Champagne to his female companions to better win them over. To this day, champagne remains synonymous with romance. Biochemists have studied its effects and conclude that it can indeed procure aphrodisiac effects, as it reduces inhibitions associated with certain areas of the brain.

Vitamin E

Vitamin E is a powerful tonic and helps protect tissue and blood cells. It is thought to exercise a direct and positive action on sexual function and fertility. Sometimes recommended to treat impotence, it has been called the reproduction vitamin. It is found in most vegetable oils and in particular in wheat germ and sunflower oils and in oils from all of the nut varieties. Oats, spinach, asparagus, parsley and dandelion also contain a good supply of vitamin E.

Vulva
External Female Genitals

The <u>mons veneris</u> is the fatty pad covering the pubic bone. It contains many nerves and is covered with pubic hair at puberty. The <u>clitoral hood</u>, or prepuce, is the joining of the hairless inner lips (labia minora) over the clitoris. The clitoral hood can accumulate <u>smegma</u>, a waxy substance, which can be prevented by pulling back the hood when washing. The <u>clitoris</u> is a highly sensitive structure composed of a shaft and a glans. It contains small spongy structures which engorge with blood during sexual arousal. It's only function is pleasure. The <u>vestibule</u> is the area of the vulva (external female genitals) inside the labia minora. The <u>perineum</u> is the smooth skin between the anus and the vaginal opening. The <u>anus</u> is the opening to the rectum. The <u>labia majora</u>, the outer lips of the vulva, are covered with pubic hair. The <u>labia minora</u>, the inner lips which surround the vulva, contain extensive blood vessels and nerve endings. The <u>urethral opening</u> is used for passing urine. The <u>introitus</u> is the opening to the vagina. At birth the introitus may be covered with a membrane of tissue called the <u>hymen</u>.

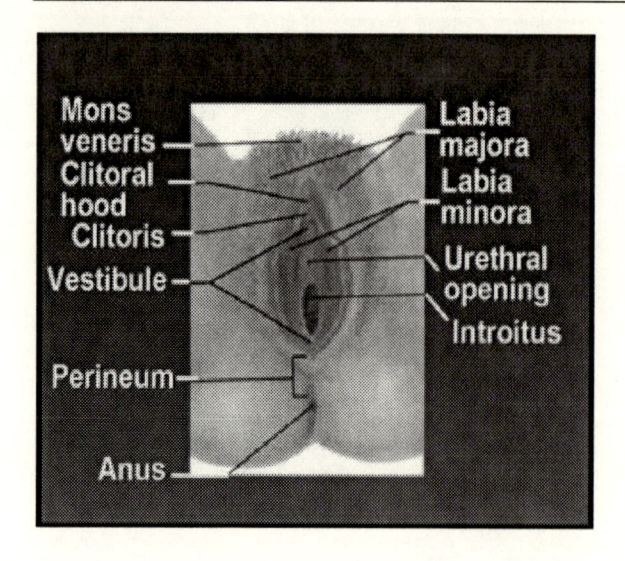

[Figure: labeled diagram of the vulva showing Mons veneris, Clitoral hood, Clitoris, Vestibule, Perineum, Anus, Labia majora, Labia minora, Urethral opening, Introitus]

Underlying Structures of the Vulva

The clitoris contains a shaft and a glans as well as the crura, which projects inward from each side of the shaft. The shaft, glans, and crura contain spongy tissue called cavernous bodies. The vestibular bulbs, now thought, by some, to be a part of the structure of the clitoris, are also filled with spongy tissue. The glans and shaft comprise only a small portion of the spongy, erectile tissue which becomes engorged with blood during sexual arousal. The function of these of these organs is solely to provide sexual arousal.

The opening to the vagina in this illustration makes it appear as an open hole, but that is because the labia minora are held apart to illustrate the vaginal opening or introitus. The urethral opening is inside the labia minora and lies between the introitus and the clitoral shaft and glans.

The Masters Guide to Cunnilingus

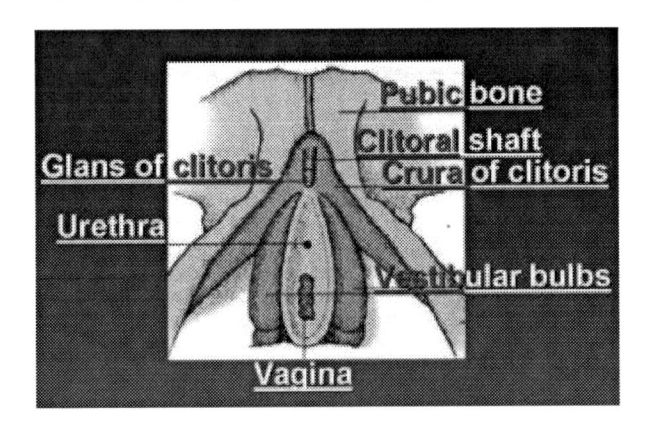

Internal Front View

The fallopian tubes are four inches long and extend from the uterus toward the ovaries. At the end of each tube are fringe-like projections called fimbriae that (after ovulation) draw the egg into the tube, where fertilization takes place. The ovaries are female gonads that produce eggs (ova) and sex hormones. The cervix is the end of the uterus in the back of the vagina.

The os is the opening in the cervix through which sperm and menstrual fluid can pass. The uterus is a pear shaped organ where a fetus can develop. The endometrium is the tissue that lines the interior wall of the uterus. The thin outside covering is the perimetrium. The smooth muscle layer of the wall is the myometrium. The vagina is a stretchable canal, about 4 inches long, that extends into the body and angles upward to the small of the back.

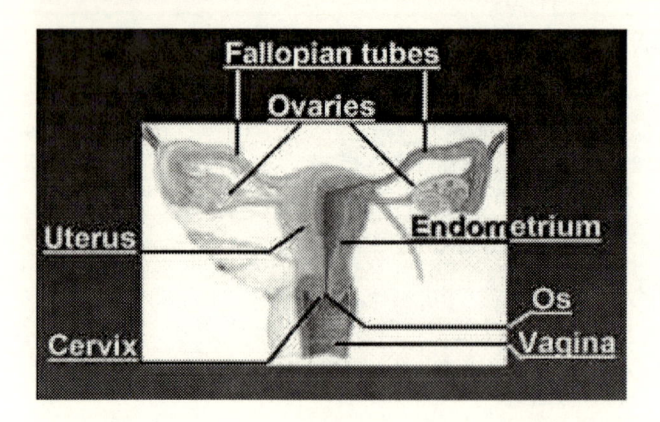

Female Reproductive and Sexual Organs

    The <u>uterus</u> is suspended in the abdominal cavity by ligaments. It is behind the vagina and between the bladder and the rectum. It is about three inches long and two inches wide in a woman who hasn't been pregnant. When a fertile egg comes from the <u>fallopian tube</u> it embeds itself in the lining, the endometrium, of the uterus. If not, some of the lining exits as <u>menstrual fluid</u> about once a month. The ovaries are the size and shape of almonds. They contain from 40,000 to 400,000 immature eggs at birth and will release about 450 lifetimes. The <u>bladder</u> is smaller than a man's, perhaps because of a possible pregnancy. The <u>clitoris</u> swells during sexual arousal. The swelling occurs in the glans, the shaft and the <u>crura</u> of the clitoris, which spread out on each side of the vagina and connect to the pubic bone. <u>Vestibular bulbs</u>, on each side of the vagina, also swell with blood during arousal and the <u>Bartholin's glands</u> secrete a few drops of fluid.

The Masters Guide to Cunnilingus

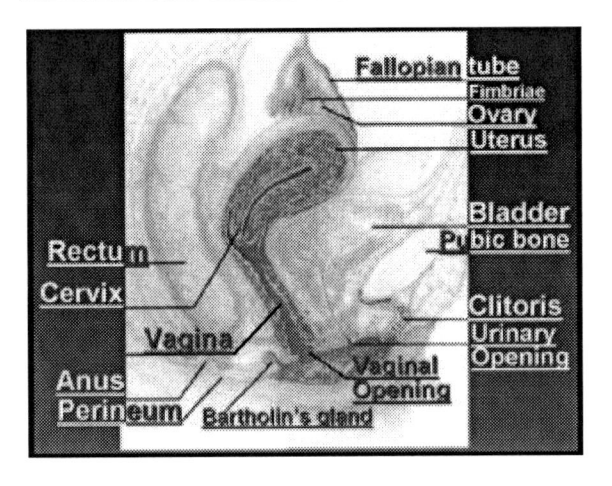

[Anatomical diagram labeled: Fallopian tube, Fimbriae, Ovary, Uterus, Bladder, Pubic bone, Clitoris, Urinary Opening, Vaginal Opening, Bartholin's gland, Perineum, Anus, Vagina, Cervix, Rectum]

The Vagina

When the <u>vagina</u> is unaroused its walls form a flat tube. The vagina is potential space, not space, when closed. It expands during sexual arousal and expands much larger during childbirth. The folded walls of the vagina, the <u>rugae</u>, are moist and warm. When arousal occurs blood flows to the cavernous bodies in the clitoris and vestibular bulbs, and lubrication of the vaginal walls occurs. The <u>speculum</u> is an instrument with two blades used to open the vaginal walls during a gynecological examination. The <u>Pap smear</u> is part of this exam. It's a test for cancer of the cervix by taking a sample of cells. There are few nerves at the back of the vagina, so this is not usually painful.

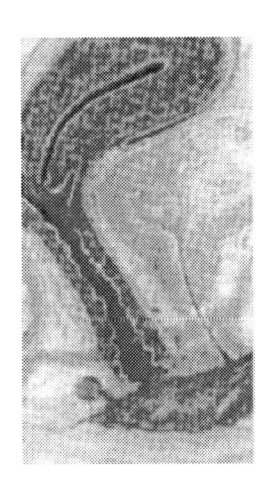

The G-Spot

The Grąfenburg spot, also known as the G spot, is an area on the front wall of the vagina named for Ernest Grąfenburg who described it in 1950. Some women have observed this spot to be an area of erotic sensitivity when given manual stimulation.

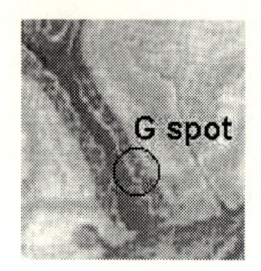

The G-Spot, the A-Spot & the Clit: An Orgasmic Combo

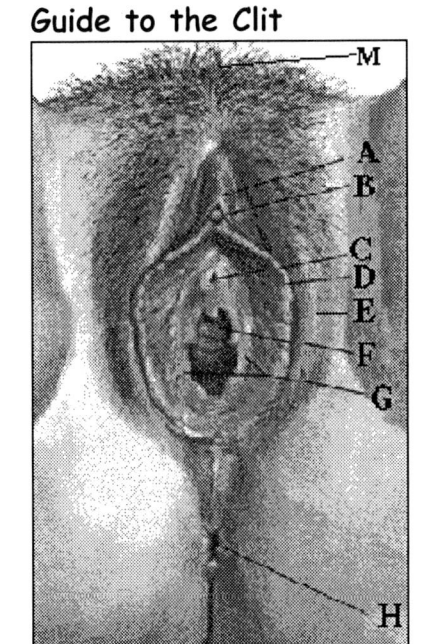

Guide to the Clit

M: Mons veneris A: Hood of Clitoris **B**: Clitoris **C**: Opening of Urethra **D**: Labia minora **E**: Labia majora **F**: Opening of Vagina **G**: Vestibule (Bartholin's) Glands **H**: Anus

Do you know where your girlfriend's clitoris is? I mean, do you *really* know? Maybe you *think* you know where her clit is...but you are wrong. That's right. Unless you are a gynecologist, chances are you do not really know how to locate a woman's clit. That is why I am going to give you a guided tour to this very important part of the female anatomy.

Searching for Hidden Treasure

The love button, the joy buzzer, the pebble in the moss, the little man in the canoe – whatever you call the clitoris, you know it is there somewhere, according to legend, but the dang thing is hard to find. Part of the problem is that anatomy can vary from woman to woman. Well, actually it does not vary that much. She is not going to have her clit under her nose. But you may not recognize her clit because it does not resemble your last girlfriend's – in size, shape, or positioning. So the first thing to know when seeking out the wild clitoris is this: every woman is different.

Let's begin the journey in the same basic area – south of the pubic triangle, north of the vagina. You do know how to find a vagina, don't you? Look upward from the vagina and you will notice two thin walls of flesh on either side of you. These are the labia minora, a.k.a. the meatflaps. Like testicles, the labia come in a variety of sizes and shapes; some women's are neat and tidy, and some have low hangers. While they are not part of the clitoris, they are attached to the skin that covers it. Pulling on them or rubbing them may be pleasurable to a woman, and some may even enjoy getting off this way if they do not like direct clitoral stimulation. But in general, the labia minora are just window dressing.

Do Not Enter

Forging up and ahead, you will encounter on the uppermost rim of the vagina, a small protuberance, where, if you look very closely, you will see a small hole. This is the urethra, otherwise known as the peehole. In general, you do not want to mess too much with the urethra, not only because it issues forth urine, but because too much poking and rubbing in this area can result in discomfort and urinary infections for the woman.

Clit

Hopefully by now, you have reached the foothills of the clitoral shaft. Yes, it is a shaft, just like your shaft, but much smaller. The clitoris is the female analog to the penis, and is filled with the same type of spongy erectile tissue as the penis. That means that it does get larger, longer, and harder when the woman becomes aroused.

At the apex of the female genitalia, shrouded by a forest of pubic hair (unless she's clear-cut her short and curlies) and walled in on either side by the labia majora (the fatty pads that press together and enclose her pussy) lies the goal. The clitoris may be hidden from direct view by folds of skin known as the prepuce or clitoral hood. Anatomically, this corresponds to the male foreskin. With 6,000 to 8,000 nerve endings, the clitoris is very sensitive and needs some buffering between it and the world (or the inside of her jeans). The skin of the clitoral hood protects the clit from direct over stimulation. When the woman is aroused, her clit may enlarge and the hood may retract, revealing the head of the clitoris. Otherwise, if she has not aroused, you may have to pull the skin back with your fingers to get to the actual clit itself.

Look Under the Hood

With the skin of the clitoral hood retracted, you will now see the button itself. It is small, smooth and round, and if you look closely you will see that it resembles an itty-bitty tiny cock head. But do not let that freak you out. Just remember that, like your penis head, this part of a woman is extremely sensitive and needs to be treated with care. Poking, prodding, rough licking, or sharp fingernails are not appreciated.

Some women do not like direct or vigorous stimulation on the tip of their clit at all. They may prefer to have the sides, i.e., the "shaft" part, stimulated. If you run your finger upward from the tip of the clit to where you hit the pubic bone, you will have traced the length of her clitoral shaft. It may feel like a firm ridge under the skin, and it will get harder and more pronounced when she is turned on. Try stroking along the sides or top of the clit shaft, or try pressing lightly with a finger and moving just the skin of the hood back and forth.

Another hot spot to try out is the underside of the clit. You know how good it feels to get the underside of your penis head worked during a blowjob? The next time you go down on her, try licking *lightly* just below and underneath the tip of her clit. Remember, do not get too close to the peehole. Or do, if you are into that kind of thing.

Since the clit hood is analogous to the foreskin – well, you know what can build up under your foreskin.

Yes, women do get the equivalent of dick cheese, or smegma, albeit in smaller and probably less smelly amounts. But if your girlfriend's vagina is less than fresh, this is one place to look for the problem. She needs to be pulling back the skin over her clit and washing underneath to get rid of the accumulating gunk.

The Secret Subterranean Clit

Now that I've thoroughly acquainted you with the topside of the clit, it's time to delve deeper. This is where things get tricky and where we enter mysterious realms you previously never dreamed existed. You see that little nub that sticks out on her – well that is really only the tip of the clit iceberg, so to speak.

Let's go further now, into the inner realms of your girlfriend's pelvis. Because that is where the rest of her clit is. Yes, the *rest* of her clit. There is more, much more, to it than that little bump on the surface, although arguably that is the most crucial part. Although the shaft and head of the clit stick out from the body only a centimeter or two, in reality the shaft extends inside the body, into the pelvis, about 7 to 9 centimeters (3 to 4 inches). Like the above-ground clit, the rest of the shaft is made of the same erectile tissue, which gets hard and engorged during arousal.

The clitoris keeps going and going. Branching out from the main shaft, and running along either side of the vagina (this is an inch or two under the skin) are the two "legs" of the internal clitoris. Imagine a wishbone shape, with the top of the wishbone being the tip of the clit, and the two sides forking down around the vagina. These branches are also made of spongy tissue that engorges when the woman gets aroused. This is good, because it increases blood flow to her genitals, and it may also put a bit more of a squeeze on the inner sides of her vagina. Also, just beneath the labia minora lie two "bulbs" that are also part of the clitoral structure. When they get enlarged, they harden the walls of the vagina, which scientists think may help facilitate intercourse.

Some doctors who have studied the clit in detail say that the elusive G-spot may also be connected to or part of the clit. The G-spot, more clinically called the urethral sponge, is another mass of spongy tissue that surrounds the woman's urethra and sits on the top side of the vagina just beneath the clit. You can stimulate the G-spot most easily by pressing up against the top inner vaginal wall, angling toward the belly button. The G-spot feels like a rough bump about the size of half a walnut. For some women, pressing on this spot just makes them feel like they need to pee. But for others, it creates mind-blowing orgasms, which in some cases turn into gushing geysers of female ejaculation.

Applying Your Knowledge

Now that you have gotten to know the clit inside and out, how can you take your newfound knowledge home and apply it in the bedroom? For one thing, now that you know how much of the clit is inside and around a woman's vagina, you may want to reevaluate your technique for finger fucking and thrusting. The good old in-and-out is not really going to do that much for her. You have to work that thing – move it around in there and stir things up. Move it side to side, up and down, every which way. I do not mean you should be poking directly at her vaginal walls – just try applying a little more pressure laterally with your strokes, and try to bump into the G-spot when you can.

Of course, knowing that there is so much more to the clit than meets the eye is no excuse for neglecting the main attraction. The part of the clit that we see and know and love is still the most active and sensitive part of the female sex organs and it needs to keep getting all the attention you can give it. But now you can see that what appeared to be just a fleshy nub is really more complex. It has a sensitive tip and underside, a shaft, and a hood covering it all. You can try focusing on any or all of these parts of the clit when you finger or eat out your girlfriend. Try a little of this and a little of that and see how she responds.

Now that you have got your basic roadmap to the clitoris, keep exploring. Every woman is different and unique, so take the time to really learn your way around your favorite pussy. Your best sexual adventures are still ahead of you.

The G-Spot

Before we start our journey further into the depths of the female pleasure palace, let me give you a little background on the G-spot and why it is considered a prime destination. Discovery of the G-spot is attributed to sex researcher Dr. Ernest Grafenberg (G-spot is short for Grafenberg spot). Of course, women have always had G-spots, but until Grafenberg's studies of female orgasm in the 1950s, apparently no one was paying attention or realized there was a certain place in the vagina that when stimulated, made women come, and come hard.

The G-spot is sort of the female equivalent of the prostate gland in males. In women, this structure is called the urethral sponge, and like the prostate, it surrounds a portion of the urethra before it exits the body. In men, the prostate is stimulated by pressing on the anterior (front) wall of the rectum. In women, it can be reached from within the vagina.

And just as stimulating the prostate can enhance orgasm and ejaculation for men, stimulating the G-spot can greatly boost orgasm for the woman, creating a more intense climax, and in some cases, female ejaculation.

Get the Feel for It

Part of the reason the G-spot is so hard to find is that you can not see it. You have to feel it, and even then, you have to seek it out under the right conditions. It is located about two inches inside the vaginal canal, on the upper (front) surface of the vaginal wall. The G-spot gets engorged and enlarged when a woman is sexually excited, so it is easiest to find it once your woman is already turned on. It is also not really sensitive to stimulation until a woman is already aroused, so there is no point in poking at it until you get her primed a bit first. Here is where your expert knowledge of the clitoris, gained from your previous reading, will come in handy. Work her clit, and get her wet and ready before you go diving in for the G.

To locate the G-spot, turn your palm upward to face the ceiling and insert two fingers into her vagina. Feel the upper surface of the vaginal wall for a rough-feeling bump about the size of a half a walnut.

The surface here may feel kind of ridged, like the roof of your mouth just behind your front teeth. If you insert your fingers all the way into her vagina, then bend them slightly like you are beckoning someone towards you and start to pull them out, your fingertips should bump right into and come to rest on the G-spot. It should feel firm, but a little squishy.

Put the Pressure On

The G-spot responds to firm pressure, not light petting. Once you find it, you have to dig in and really rub on it. Slow, deep, steady strokes are best. Before you put any heavy pressure on the G-spot, spread your fingers apart slightly. Imagine a clock face around the vagina, with the clit at high noon. Position your fingers so they correspond to 11 o'clock and 1 o'clock. The urethra is directly in line with the 12 o'clock position, so you do not want to put hard pressure on that, because it can cause irritation and discomfort. Stimulating the G-spot will often initially produce a feeling of needing to urinate. This is normal, and you will know you are pressing on the right area when she tells you she feels like she has to pee. In fact, it is a good idea to have her empty her bladder before you begin, so she can relax and this will not be a concern.

To stroke the G-spot, hook the fingers upward and pull towards you. This should move the G-spot into contact with the pubic bone. The G-spot will then be compressed between the pubic bone and your fingers. Slide your fingers out part way, keeping firm pressure against the spot. As you slide your fingers back in, nudge against the G-spot with the flat part of your fingers. Do not poke at it with your fingertips. Repeat the "come here" motion with your fingers as you stroke in and out. Another way to stimulate the G-spot is to do a gentle squeeze-and-release massage. Locate the G-spot and compress it against the inside of the pubic bone as described above. Then use your fingers to press and release the spot rhythmically, "milking" it. You can also keep steady pressure on the spot and slowly rock your fingers back and forth, pulling them toward you slightly, and then moving them away from you. Try a few different strokes and see what elicits the best response.

Bringing It All Together

Although massaging the G-spot can greatly intensify a woman's orgasm, G-spot stimulation alone is usually not enough to make her come. For this reason, it is important to maintain some kind of clitoral stimulation while you are working on her G.

You can do this with your thumb, with your other hand, with your mouth, or you can have her touch her own clit while you focus on exploring her inner passage. Having her touch herself may be the best option when you are starting out, since it takes a bit of skill and concentration to coordinate stroking her G-spot and petting her clit at once.

As you are pressing on her G-spot and her arousal builds, it should feel slightly different to her than clitoral stimulation alone. The feelings may seem deeper and more intense. The feeling of having to pee should go away, and be replaced by a pleasurable warmth and an urgency to climax. When she comes, the orgasm may be much stronger than what she usually experiences. Do not be surprised if her whole body writhes and contracts with sweet convulsions of ecstasy.

Making Her Squirt

Also, do not be surprised if you find a big damp spot on the sheets. It does not mean she wet the bed (although she probably did complain of feeling like she had to pee). Stimulating a woman's G-spot can lead to female ejaculation, a gush of fluid produced by the glands around the G-spot area that you have been pressing on. Stroking the G-spot gets these glands engorged and primed, and the longer you stroke, the juicier they get.

When she comes, the contractions can force those fluids out. Because the liquid comes out of the urethra, there has been some controversy over whether female ejaculation is a real phenomenon, or if it is just urine that is getting expelled during orgasm. However, researchers who have analyzed female ejaculatory fluid say it is different than urine, although it may include a small amount of urine if there is a residual amount in the urethra at the time of ejaculation.

When you first begin to explore the G-spot, you do not have

to make female ejaculation a goal. It is not likely to happen the first time, but as you become more familiar with the G-spot and how to stimulate it, you can work up to trying for an ejaculation. The trick is to prolong the stimulation as long as possible before she climaxes, to really get the juices primed. If the glands are really swollen, she may feel like she is going to pee as she climaxes. Tell her to just let it go and bear down and push out with her pelvic muscles. This will help release and expel the built up fluids. It's a good idea to put a towel under her beforehand to soak up the wetness, and it will make her less worried about having an accident.

Including the G-spot in sex takes a little extra effort and concentration, so you probably will not want to seek out her special zone for every session. But when you do, brace yourself for bed-shaking, teeth-rattling, digging-her-fingernails-into-your-back climaxes.

You will both be rewarded by the work that goes into finding her G-spot and waking it up...although the neighbors may not appreciate it when her orgasmic screaming wakes them up.

The A-Spot. Another G-Spot

Where is it ?

The A-Spot is supposed to be situated on the front wall of the vagina, about one third down, below the cervix. It was discovered by chance in 1996, during an experiment designed to find a remedy for vaginal dryness. The researchers then discovered that 95% of the women tested became very aroused when this area was stimulated. Numerous women have experienced their first orgasm this way, or have discovered that this kind of orgasm is much more intense than an orgasm obtained in the more traditional way.

Taste & Smell of the "Love Flowers"

Women often worry that their genitals will have an unpleasant odor. Some women are uncomfortable with receiving oral pleasure because it is difficult for them to accept their own genitals as being attractive to their partner. They worry about whether they will taste or smell unpleasant to their partner. It is usually enhances a woman's arousal during oral sex if she feels that her vagina, clitoris, pubic hair and vaginal lips are clean and beautiful. If a woman has not accepted this part of her body as attractive, she usually winds up with a mixed set of feelings. On the one hand she is aroused and stimulated, on the other hand she worries about "down there" not being acceptable or a turn-on. There are many women who love the beauty of their vaginas from the way they look to the way they smell, however many women also feel negative about their "love flowers".

Let her know that you love eating her pussy out. Pretend her vagina is a cherry lollipop that you are dying to lick. You love the way she smells. You are not giving her oral sex for her pleasure...you are giving her oral sex for your pleasure. You eat her pussy is its own reward. She will know that you are a master at the art of cunnilingus. She will need to hear from her man that he enjoys her vagina's natural taste and scent, and that far from finding it unpleasant, he actually likes it.

If you are with a woman and planning on performing oral sex on her she may need reassurance that her genitals are beautiful, unique and a real turn on for you. Sex will be more pleasurable for her if she is relaxed and feels you are turned on by what you are doing. Most men really like the natural taste and scent of a woman's vagina. In fact, it's often very sexually arousing for them.

However, if the taste or smell really bothers you or is a concern, ask her to wash first. There are times when the vulva may smell or taste unpleasant. This may result when the normal moisture from the vagina collects in the folds of the vulva. As a result of poor air circulation around the genitals, evaporation of excess moisture cannot occur. Since bacteria love warm moist places, they can reproduce rapidly in this environment, resulting in a strong odor, and perhaps taste. The bacteria cause the odor, not the vaginal moisture. Since women today generally wear clothing that prevents adequate circulation of air around their genitals, it may be necessary for a woman to rinse her genitals with plain water prior to engaging in oral sex. A thorough cleaning is a must. Most people who enjoy cunnilingus agree that a clean vagina is a good, if acquired, taste. A good vigorous shower will do much to neutralize the taste of your partner. You can start with a thorough and luxurious bath or shower together, cleaning each other carefully and gently. Soap up her vulva, washing between her outer and inner lips. Spread her lips apart and gently wash her clitoris. Hey, don't stop - this feels great! Run your soapy hand down the crack of her ass, and rub a finger all around her anus. You can stick one finger in and wash around inside too, if you anticipate any anal play, and I suggest you do. But don't put those soapy fingers up her vagina. Instead, rinse them off well and stick one or two inside, making a circular motion. Think about washing the inside of a tall glass - same thing. Now wasn't that fun? And now you can feel free to let your tongue wander anywhere it pleases...

Make sure you tell her how much you love her taste. Tell her your mouth is watering at the very thought of licking her vagina. Mention how much you love to lick away at her clit. The more comfortable she feels about having you go down on her, the more relaxed she'll be. It's much easier for a woman to orgasm when she's relaxed.

Cunnilingus Licking & Eating Pussy

Head (cunnilingus) or refers to stimulation of a woman's genitals with her partner's mouth. This can include sucking or licking the outer and inner areas of the vagina, and most often involves direct stimulation of the clitoris. Some women find cunnilingus the most satisfying part of sex. Indeed, a great number of women say oral sex is the only way they can achieve orgasm. The mouth can create a uniquely intense range of sensations which many find unrivaled. It has been said that while there are many men who can do the job sexually, there are very few who are experts in the art of cunnilingus. Women will do virtually anything for a man who can bring them to countless orgasms with his tongue alone. In fact, for many women, cunnilingus is the only way they can experience orgasm. Cunnilingus is perhaps the most enjoyed form of partner sex women engage in. Nothing can compare to the feeling of a warm wet tongue sliding across a woman's vulva and clitoris. With the exception of masturbation, oral sex probably results in more female orgasms than any other sexual practice.

Cunnilingus might be her preferred form of stimulation

because the lips and tongue of a lover are softer and more sensitive than fingers, a toy, a penis, or dildo. It can be part of your lovemaking buffet, foreplay or the main event that culminates in orgasm. For women who do not usually get off this way, it might be a fun pleasure experiment to see what works, and what does not. You can make the experience into anything you want. The key to performing good oral sex on a female is to talk to your partner, check it out with her, what feels good, what she likes and does not enjoy, listen to her breathing patterns and body responses. Learning to go down on a woman means understanding her pleasure anatomy -- but it also requires trust, lust, and communication between both partners, no matter if it is a one night stand or a ten-year relationship. With a little trust and a dose of horniness, the possibilities for orgasmic cunnilingus are endless. Performing cunnilingus can be one of the most wonderful things you can do for a woman. It makes her feel loved, admired, sexy, and has the potential to give her an exceptional orgasm. Many women prefer it to intercourse, and for those who require a large amount of clitoral stimulation, it is the easiest way to orgasm. Besides, lots of women expect it these days and men who perform great cunnilingus are always appreciated and considered fabulous lovers.

Cunnilingus is a delicate skill, requiring patience, practice, and dedication to get it right, but any woman you learn to do it right for will appreciate you all the more for it.

Feeling comfortable

There are two things which should accompany you any time that you engage in oral sex: being comfortable with yourself and your partner, and your ability to communicate.

If you feel uncomfortable about performing or receiving oral sex, do not do it. It is better to stop, relax and communicate about your feeling with your partner before you begin. Oral sex involves very intimate areas, in the most intimate ways. It explores tastes, smells and feelings unlike any other form of lovemaking. Feeling comfortable about your body and your partner may take time, and you should take all the time you need. The results will be better for both of you.

Good Communication

You will never know what your partner wants or finds satisfying unless you talk to them. Sometimes if it is your first time with a particular partner communication may seem uncomfortable. Do not worry.

Do you really think that your new partner will be annoyed or upset if you ask her what she wants? A vast majority of women will be quite pleased. Do not be discouraged if you partner offers you advice; be overjoyed because you are learning what they find pleasurable which will make you a better lover as a result. A sense of humor is another great way to ease any tension which may exist between new lovers. A light hearted approach to your sexual encounter will make it more enjoyable for both of you.

Start Psychological

Start with the mental aspect. It is a vastly underrated element of a woman's sexuality and is almost completely misunderstood by the male species. Many women are self conscious about the way they taste and/or smell, especially when experimenting with a new partner. Tell her how much you are looking forward to tasting her sweet juices. Tell her you love the taste - it really turns you on. Tell her you are going to devour every last drop she has to offer. Tell her that you are good at it and you can not wait to show off your skills. Tell her all these things and anything else you can think of along the same lines. You want her to be comfortable sticking her crotch into your mouth, so it is best to lay the groundwork with some sweet talking.

Clean Up Before and After

It is a very good idea to get her good and cleaned up before embarking on any serious cunnilingus. Take a shower or bath and make sure to thoroughly wash and rinse the vaginal lips, the clitoris (wash under the hood) and the vaginal opening. Not only can this be very pleasurable, it will greatly enhance the experience for both parties. She will no longer have to worry about her body and you will certainly benefit from the cleaning.

Afterward, both of you can end up pretty messy so it is important to clean up right away. Cunnilingus juices do not age well with time, so make sure to thoroughly wash all of them off your bodies. It is also a good idea to brush your teeth and/or rinse with mouthwash. Make sure to get any straggling pubes that may have wedged their way in between your teeth.

Techniques to better cunnilingus

Clitoral Cunnilingus

The clitoris is the only organ on a woman's body that exists for the sole purpose of sexual pleasure. Hard wired for orgasm, the clit is the key to unlocking a woman's deepest erotic zones.

There is a tremendous amount of variety among women as to how much stimulation of their clit that they can stand. Some women shudder at the lightest touch while others demand that you suck on it like a clogged straw. You will need to experiment a bit when you are just getting to know a woman's sexual preferences, so start softly and work your way up. You will know it if you go past her threshold.

The clitoris is central to female sexual arousal, as it contains most of the sexually charged tissues in the body. The logical first step for many lovers, therefore, is to directly stimulate the clitoris right off the bat. The catch is many women will not be very responsive to this jump-for-the-clitoris approach. You may want to try taking things slow at first, kissing and licking her stomach and thighs, then the area around her clitoris. Build her arousal level slowly, gradually increasing pressure and speed with your mouth. Once you know she is aroused (i.e. if she's told you or motioned so) you can move to the clitoris.

Many women enjoy a massage of the mons. The mons in the mound of skin which is found on top the pubic bone above the vaginal opening. Take one or both of your hands and carefully move the mons and surrounding area much the same way you would massage someone's shoulders. Be careful not to press too hard or make too wide a circular movement. As you manually stimulate the mons, you can move your mouth to the vulva. When touching her vulva with your tongue, you may wish to concentrate solely on the clitoris after some stimulation of the labia or you may wish to lick the surrounding areas. Some women need constant clitoral stimulation to reach orgasm so ask your partner what she would have you do. Clitoral stimulation can be exciting but don't be too eager. The way that you use your tongue is important. Some women will want rapid motions of continuous licking while others prefer long, slow caresses. If you are interested you might want to try a flavored lubricant.

Add Some Flavor

A talented gourmet could work almost limitless flavors into the mix here. Whipped cream is always a fan favorite, but have you ever tried a swollen clit covered in melting ice cream? Chocolate syrup can be fun but it is messy and if it gets into the anal area - well, let's just say that can be messy and nasty. Many women have reported that the temperature and textue of jello is very erotic, while others prefer warmer treats, such as soup. Do not be afraid to experiment as the right ingredients can turn you into a hungry eater, just what every woman wants.

Start cunnilingus very gently

Kissing a girl's genitals can be a very exciting and satisfactory experience for both. It requires a certain skill, as in ordinary kissing, which means it should not cause irritation or be boring. It is important to use enough saliva on the tongue, to start off very gently and with a lot of sincere attention. Slow and teasing movements of the tongue across the vagina and around the clitoris and back can be varied with tiny quick fluttering of the tip of the tongue across the clitoris.

You can let your finger play around as well, very gently and with loving care. Do not suddenly penetrate the vagina; do not become mechanical or rough. Pay attention to how she reacts, because it is an indication of how she likes it, and if she is warming up. If she just lies there, maybe she is not enjoying it very much. Perhaps she is not ready for it, or perhaps she feels isolated. While kissing her genitals, you can still keep in touch by caressing her body, or holding her hands. You can recognize the signs of an approaching climax, and then it is best not to change your position or technique. For her to reach the climax it is important to get the same intense stimulus for at least half a minute or so.

Gentle Stroking

Once you have got her naked, begin with some soft stroking of her inner thighs. Stay away from her vagina, but let every soft stroke get tantalizingly closer and closer. Direct the strokes from the knees towards the vagina. This may tickle her a little, but she will love every minute.

Positioning

Position yourself comfortably so that your mouth is comfortably at clit level. You can be in any number of positions, but it is important that you are both comfortable. I highly recommend the laying flat position for beginners as it is easy and intuitive. Once you are set, begin by softly kissing the outer lips of the vagina. Work your way around, teasing the lips with your tongue.

First Contact

As you reach the clitoris, dart your tongue in from underneath the clit and give it a good lick from the base to the tip. This will give you a good indication of how much direct clitoral stimulation she can take at this point. Try circling the clit for a while to get her rolling. Keep stimulating the area around the clit and the clit itself until she can take direct stimulation. For some women, this will be immediate, for others, you will need to tease the area a bit before she can handle the direct contact.

Engage the Clitoris

Most of the time, you can actually feel the clitoris harden and swell with blood. This is a sign to you that it is time to focus on her pleasure button. Once you begin working hard on the clitoris, you can use a variety of techniques, but do not take your lips, tongue and mouth away from it. It is vital that you give the clit constant attention. You will find that some women like different types of strokes than others, but, for the most part, you can simply wail away with your tongue back and forth across the clitoris to get the job done. Or lick it like a thirsty dog lapping at an ice cream cone.

The Home Stretch

Many women will start to buck and moan at this point. Their legs may start shaking and many will actually start thrusting their vagina deeper into your mouth. In some cases they are trying to position their clit just right on your tongue, but most of the time they are just enjoying the ride. In any case, this is the time to really dig in, intensify your efforts and go after the clitoris until she's spent. Try a clitoral blowjob or some tongue fucking when she is deep within the throes of ecstasy and she is likely to go over the edge with a mind blowing clitoral orgasm.

Large percentage of women become hyper-sensitive in the clitoral area just after orgasm. Even the tiniest touch can be painful. Most will push you away from the area when they're through. Don't sweat it. Your work is done.

Cunnilingus and orgasm

The clitoris becomes bigger and stiffer as it gets aroused, just like a penis. At a high level of excitement, but before the orgasm, the clitoris retreats. This is not a sign of diminishing interest, on the contrary. Licking around the clitoris, keeping the tongue and lips very wet, and then concentrating on the same area with a regular and constant rhythm while perhaps playing around very lightly with a finger, will probably bring about her orgasm within a minute.

Normally speaking, an orgasm is very noticeable, because the girl is hot, covered in a thin layer of sweat, often shows a red flush all over her body, moves uncontrollably, moans or gives other vocal signals and then utters a deep explosive sigh as the peak of sexual pleasure washes over her. You recognize the signs because of your experience with yourself. The orgasm consists of 5-10 contractions of the muscles of the vagina and the anus, which can clearly be felt. Some extra moisture may come out during orgasm.

This is sometimes referred to as 'female ejaculation'. After the great orgasm tell her you really ca not believe how good it was and how much you enjoyed it. Trust me, she will be back. Believe me she will want more.

Cunnilingus and individual stimuli

If you realize that the effect of your effort is small, ask if there is perhaps something you should do differently. She may have a special technique to which she has got accustomed during masturbation. In general, individuals show some small differences in behavior, and thus often require individual stimuli. Always check if she likes what you are doing. The most typical problem of oral sex can be a sense of isolation in the receiving partner. Therefore it is very good to keep in touch with each other. Eye contact is not easy, although intermittently looks and other signals of communication can be exchanged. Touching is quite possible, caressing or holding hands, stroking or grabbing hair. So there are ways of keeping up the communication and not losing sight of each other.

Cunnilingus and hygiene

Positions must be comfortable. The kisser can avoid a stiff neck by placing a pillow under the girl's buttocks, or adopting a position where she sits on his face. Good hygiene is required. Too much hair can be unpleasant and should be trimmed. Hygiene also requires that the kisser do not move form anus to vagina with the tongue or finger, because that may transport bacteria and cause infection. If you are not certain about the partner's safety, a lick patch, made of latex or other material and provided with a flavor, can be used. Those with experience or a sense of adventure can make licking even more exciting by changing posture or clothes or by smearing tasteful substances like whipped cream or honey.

Essential Tongue Techniques & Exercises

You are expected to be able to perform for extended periods of time. In order to develop marathoner-like endurance, there are a number of exercises that can be used to strengthen the muscles in your mouth. A lot of women might take 60 minutes OR MORE before they reach the heights of ecstasy. Yes, you heard me right. 60 minutes or more! So be patient. Expect to linger in the palace a while. Unfortunately for the woman receiving the stimulation, what often gets overlooked is the actual way the tongue is being used to arouse her. The partner often is so focused on covering all the genital parts and exploring that he forgets that it is not only what is being touched, but the way it is being touched that is critical. Thus, to begin any kind of detailed discussion on cunnilingus requires a discussion on tongue usage. There are six primary types of tongue positions. Each tongue position has its own unique role in the art of love making, and of course, its own special exercise program to strengthen not only the tongue muscles, but a person's voluntary control over its usage. Unless you want to wear crutches in your mouth, developing a hardy tongue is key.

Strength requires exercise. The following exercise will allow your tongue to last for as long as you need it to, allowing you to give her prolonged, orgasmic pleasure she's felt with no man before.

Like an athlete, use this same body building exercise to "warm up" your tongue before sex. The six primary types of tongue positions used in cunnilingus are the following:

The sharp, wide tongue: To achieve this position, stick your tongue as far out of your mouth as possible, then try to touch your nose. Once you are in this position, hold the same muscle groups still and begin moving your tongue around. Practice five sets of three, moving the tongue first in circular motions, then up and down.

The sharp, round tongue: To achieve this position, point your tongue while simultaneously trying to make the top of your tongue touch the roof of your mouth and the bottom of your tongue touch the bottom of your mouth. Once you are in this position, practice moving your tongue in and out of your mouth while keeping the tongue hard and round. For the more advanced student, try keeping your mouth closed and circling your tongue around inside of it, while of course, maintaining position.

Flat, soft, wide tongue: To achieve this position, flatten your tongue in your mouth. Try to make your tongue rest gently on the bottom teeth. Once you have accomplished this, slowly, while holding the position, move your tongue outside the mouth. Practice curling the wide tip of the tongue upward, downward and side to side. This too, practice for five sets of three, while holding each move for 2 seconds.

Flat, hard, wide tongue: To achieve this position, flatten your tongue in your mouth. Cover all your bottom teeth with your mouth. Using some force, try to explode your tongue in all the side positions. Using all the muscles in your tongue, try to move your tongue around. Move it both in and out of your mouth, while maintaining the position of evenly wide and hard.

Upside down tongue: To achieve this position, turn your tongue upside down in your mouth. Then try sticking it outside of your mouth, all the while maintaining the position.

Side curled tongue: To achieve this position, curl the two sides of your tongue until the two sides of your tongue touch each other. Then stick your tongue outside of your mouth. While maintaining position, practice circling your tongue clockwise and counter-clockwise.

Keeping Tongue Moist

While using your tongue to touch your own arm or your partner's vulva that your tongue may soon feel dry. This frequently happens and in fact, tongue position often is irrelevant. However, there is a simple technique that you can use to eliminate this situation. Begin the lick with the tip of your tongue being moist/slightly wet from your own saliva. After a few minutes of touching your partner, your mouth will naturally start producing saliva. The key thing here is to always keep your tongue moist, without drooling. One of the worst things is for a partner to play to rough on the genital area. That is why it is good to practice the different amounts of saliva necessary on your own arm first. Some people like to use flavored oils on the partner's vulva while doing these exercises which can be especially rewarding for a hard workout well done.

Lubrication helps things continue to feel smooth. If you are having difficulty balancing the art of salivating but not drooling, try buying some flavored oils.

The next time that the two of you are together, try switching your tongue positions and see how that influences her reaction to your forms of touch.

Starting Licks

Your woman tastes like a sweet peach and you enjoy nothing more than setting yourself up in a comfortable position to give her a tongue lashing every now and then. Now that your tongue is in shape it's time to start licking. Lick everything you can get your tongue on and are legally allowed to touch. You can not go down there only to reciprocate or worse, hoping that it will encourage her to pay your manhood a visit -- you should want to be there. Encouraging sounds like "mmm," "ooh" and "aah" will make her feel like you're enjoying the act. And you should be enjoying it.

Any licking and sucking of the labia, vaginal entrance, clitoris, or anal area is going to feel just great. Start your tonguing by lapping her vulva from vaginal entrance up to her clitoris, while keeping your tongue and jaw relaxed. Run your tongue between the inner and outer labia on one side, while keeping the two sides together between your lips.

(There are two lips on each side of her vulva, do this to one side at a time.) Then do the other side. Repeating this technique going up and down and vice versa can be a great opener. Nothing heightens a sexual experience like taking things slowly. Start out with small, slow strokes of the tongue and gradually make the strokes longer, but keep the pace slow at all times. Be careful to not apply too much pressure on the clitoris in the beginning, wait for her signal - moaning and bucking her hips. This drives some women wild, and others can't take it.

Labial Hold

While holding the two parts together with your lips, run your tongue between the inner and outer labia one side at a time. Don't hold it too long - labia need to breathe.

Tongue Intercourse

The majority of a woman's nerve endings in her vagina are

The Masters Guide to Cunnilingus

around the opening and within the first couple of inches inside, or she may have them in an adorable leather pouch in her purse. Target them with your tongue, acquiring the target with your heads-up display. Insert your munitions. This technique, like life itself, is limited due to length.

Use a strong tongue

Instead of keeping your tongue relaxed whilst tickling her pink, opt instead to give your tongue that razor's edge by making it pointy and licking her all over the area. Soft is nice, but hard can be fantastic for her.

Use fingers

While the tongue is great and, well, necessary for oral sex, throwing a couple of fingers into the mix will definitely up the ante, so to speak. Use your clean, nail-trimmed finger to manipulate her body from the inside, while your tongue continues to do its thing on the outside. Multiple sensations may lead to other multiples.

Play with her butt

In the spirit of fingers, while your index finger is finding its way inside her vagina, use your thumb to simply rub the rim of her anus. If she reacts in a very positive way, wet a finger with her juices and slowly insert your finger into her anus. But remember; once that finger goes in the back way, you shouldn't put it in the front again.

Massage while you eat

You are not restricted to the genital area of her body; you can periodically use your hands to hold on to her waist and hips, and you can always manipulate her nipples with your fingers while your mouth is busy at work below. As well, you can massage her butt cheeks, rub her thighs, or even play with her ankles and feet.

Spread those lips

Use your hands to spread her labia apart and lightly flick your tongue against her clitoris while the cool air does its thing to keep it cool. As well, lightly massage her outer labia with your fingertips periodically.

Penetrate her with your tongue

You've spent so much time catering to the outskirts of her honey, now it's time to move on in. Point your tongue and make it as hard as you can (like an erection of sorts), and slowly penetrate her with it, slowly going as deep as you can.

Close those lips

Lightly squeeze her outer lips together so that her inner lips form a closed mouth and start off by licking one side to completion, and then the other. Let go of her lips, wait a moment, and start all over again.

Suck that clitoris

When she's well on her way to flowing pleasure, take her entire clitoris into your mouth and slowly suck on it, all the while constantly rubbing your tongue against it. Remember to take your time and keep your ears open for her reaction.

Use a mint

Whether you opt for Altoids (the curiously strong mint) or Halls (the black variety), placing a mint in your mouth whilst arousing her love button will provide that cooling sensation we all love so much (blowing air is not necessary). Pop a mint into your mouth and get to work. And if you're lucky, she'll do the same.

The Masters Guide to Cunnilingus

Alternate between mouth and manhood

Give her a piece of oral and penile penetration by alternating between your tongue and your penis. Lick up a storm for a while, and then make your way up to kiss her while inserting your manhood into her. Withdraw after a minute, get back down there and eat some more, then penetrate again. Keep her guessing all the while.

Intense vulva techniques for intense orgasm

When she is really hot and her vulva is throbbing try these incredible intense techniques. Watch her signals closely as these techniques may be too much, even when she is nearing orgasm. With her clitoris still exposed, give it a quick little suck by pulling it into your mouth briefly and letting it go. This will drive her insane with ecstasy! Take her exposed clitoris into your mouth and gently suck on it, at the same time flick your tongue over and around her clit. This can be done very lightly or very aggressively, and combined with fingering, will usually rapidly produce an intense orgasm. Try rolling your tongue into a tube by bringing the sides of your tongue up and together. If you can not do this with your tongue, you can not learn it, it is a genetic trait. Roll your tongue into a tube around the shaft of her clitoris, sliding it up and down, making a tiny vulva of your own for her clitoris to fuck.

Golden Fingers: The Double Pleasure Clamp Rules

Simply thrusting your fingers into and out of a vagina looks like fun if you're watching a porno movie, but is unlikely to produce any real pleasure for the woman. The first thing to remember is to keep the vagina properly lubricated. Even if you're using some sort of lubricant on the area, it's best to start slow and let her natural lubricating juices develop. Light clitoral stimulation along with some sexy talk or fantasy foreplay will usually get the job done.

Of course there is always the popular "come here" motion that you make with your pointer finger to effectively stimulate the g-spot. Using pressure up into the g-spot is highly effective and often more desirable than just light rubbing. However, let's take a look at some more innovative fingering techniques to use with oral stimulation.

The Double Pleasure Clamp Techniques

These Clamp techniques are quite effective pleasure techniques:

1) The Clamp with Oral Stimulation
Stimulates the clit using the thumb and your tongue, while using one or more fingers to stimulate the g-spot. A good technique when you are able to be in front of a woman. Most women prefer one to two fingers, although some women like a lot of pressure and three to four can be used as well.

2) The Two-fingered Clamp With Oral Stimulation
This is best used when a woman is on her knees or standing with her bottom outward. Her partner then uses this technique from behind her. The thumb stimulates the g-spot, and the fingers make a "V" around her clit while you lick it. You may need to position yourself under her like you are "changing her oil."

The most effective stimulation is using rhythmic thrusting. These rhythmic movements create vibrations, which induce pleasure in the cervix and uterus as well as in the G-spot and vagina. When fingers are introduced into the vaginal opening, the initial pleasure is primarily from the feeling of distention or fullness.

Advanced Oral Sex Stimulation

Circling the Clit

Locate the base of the clit with the tip of your tongue and being tracing slow circles around the base. Your tongue will frequently be rubbing up against the sides and tip of the clit as you circle - this just adds to the pleasure. Vary the speed as you go, taking her through several waves of pleasure, but always keep increasing the speed. Around and around and around you go, when she gets off, you're sure to know.

Sucking

Be very careful the first time you try sucking on a woman's clit. Some women are very sensitive and will shriek in pain. For the most part, once you've warmed her up with a little licking on the clit, place your lips gently around the clit and give a soft suck. You'll get a reaction right away. If she likes it, do it again and again, sucking a little harder and longer each time. Mix in a little jamming for an awesome combination.

Figure 8

Use the tip of your tongue to trace a figure 8 around her clit. Don't be afraid to knock the clit around a little bit as your tongue darts one way and then another. The sensations of you coming at her from all sides at once will thrill her with delight. The technique does require some skill and stamina, but the results are well worth it.

Jamming

With your lips placed on either side of her clit, jam your tongue downward repeatedly striking the clit. Don't worry if you don't hit it square on every time as the sliding sensations of your tongue battering her erect clit will send her over the wall. Act like you're using your tongue as a jackhammer to break the clit down. Mix in a little sucking for an awesome combination.

Tongue Fucking

Stiffen your tongue and thrust it deep into her vaginal opening. Wiggle the tip around a bit if you can at the point of maximum penetration. Move your head and neck back and forth so that your tongue is "fucking" the vaginal opening.

Lapping at the Vagina

A phenomenal technique for getting her warmed up is lapping your tongue across her lips, the vaginal opening and finally, the clitoris itself. Pretend you're a dog on a hot summer day licking an ice cream cone. Make appreciative noises as you're lapping away and you're likely to reward like a good little doggie. Don't be afraid to let a little spittle hang down from your chin.

Spittle

While most women provide plenty of lubrication from their own juices, it can be fun and exciting to mix a little of your own spittle into the mix. This technique is particularly effective if you are not really into the taste. As you are licking, sucking and probing around with your tongue, allow the spittle from inside your mouth to trickle down your tongue and into the vagina. The added lubrication will make your tongue super slippery as it glides across her pleasure zones.

Clitoral Blowjob

An advanced technique for those women who can handle direct stimulation of their clit is the clitoral blowjob. Begin by sucking slowly on the clitoris, as if you were giving it a tiny blowjob. Gradually increase the intensity of the sucking, and then begin to add a little flick from your tongue now and then. As she gets closer to orgasm, bring her over the edge by continuously swirling your tongue around the tip of the clit while you suck on the base of it. This one is guaranteed.

Cunnilingus Positions to Make Her Squirt

Laying Flat - There are a lot of sub variations on this particular position, as you can situate yourself many different ways to give cunnilingus to a woman who is laying on her back. A great beginner position is to have her laying flat on her back with her legs completely spread. Approach from between her feet and lay on your stomach between her legs with your lips at clit level. Another great one is to have her lay on the edge of the bed with her legs up in the air. Approach from the floor and as you put your head between her legs, let them drape over your shoulders. She can also try putting her feet up in the air, depending on how what is more comfortable.

Standing - With her standing facing you, kneel directly in front of her and position your lips at clit level. This is a great position to use your hands and fingers as they are freed up to explore. Try a little anal excitement with your fingers while your tongue is busy working her clit over.

Her Sitting - Chairs and couches provide can be stimulating accessories that allow for some unique positions. Try having her sit in a chair with arms, draping her legs over the arms. Approach from below; you should have plenty of room to maneuver.

Doggie Style - You just can't beat the view when you've got her on all fours with her back arched so her head slides down to the pillow. You can go straight in there or position yourself like a car mechanic and slide underneath to begin "servicing". This position also frees up your hands and fingers so don't be afraid to let them do a little exploring.

69 - An all time favorite, I would be remiss not to include the classic 69 position in my cunnilingus guide. The great benefit of this position is that you'll be receiving pleasure as well as giving it, so make sure you don't stop on your end. You can position yourselves in many ways (even standing), so experiment a little and find what works best for you.

Eating at the Y - Lay her flat on a table with her legs dangling off the edge. Pull up a chair directly between her legs and you're ready for lunch at the hottest diner in town. You'll have your hands and fingers free, so use them - and any handy utensils - to provide pleasure across her entire plate. Use pillows or blankets to get her comfortable as this is an easy position to operate from and can lead to longer than average cunnilingus sessions.

Face Squat - A word of warning. Any time you let a woman who is receiving oral sex position her entire body directly above your mouth, you run the risk of her practically suffocating you during orgasm. On the other hand, this position can be intensely pleasurable for her because it allows her to position herself just the way she likes it. Try stiffening her tongue and letting her ride it all the way home. You'll be surprised how many women really like this.

Innovate Positions for Cunnilingus

The classic legs Closed

How it's done:

Your partner lies on her back, but keeps her legs together instead of spread.

Advantage:

This is a good basic position, especially for women who are shy or nervous about oral sex.

Secret to Success

Try long, gentle strokes along the inside of her tights, from her knees to her pubic hair. This will help stimulate sensation in other areas and get her juices flowing well before you approach her 'action spots'.

Straight on, variation 1

How it's done:

Your partner lies on her back with her legs over your shoulders. You on your stomach with your face between her legs. Put a pillow under her hips and beneath your chest to reduce the stress on your neck.

Advantage:

This position is ideal for women who prefer a strong, upward stroking motion with the more textured top surface of your tongue.

Secret to success:

Try using your hands to push gently upward on her abdomen, stretching her skin away from her pubic bone. This stretching action often heightens the sensation created by your tongue strokes.

Straight on, variation 2

How it's done:

Starting from the same position as in variation 1, have your partner pull on leg upward, so that her thigh rests on or alongside her chest.
 Use your arm to hold it in position when she starts squirming.

Advantage:

In this variation, her vagina will be much more open, facing upward, so your face is in more of a downward position – which should be easier on your neck. This open position is great for women who enjoy very strong, very direct clitoral stimulation.

Secret to success:

With gravity in your favor, you will find that saliva builds in your mouth. Use it. Things can get uncomfortable for her if your tongue starts to dry out.

Loving the prize

How it's done:

With your partner on her back, position yourself so that you are lying over her at an angle.

Your chest will be resting against her abdomen with your head facing the foot of the bed (your face will be nose-down in her genitalia). Use one arm to reach around her thigh, and gently part her labia from beneath.

Advantage:

In this position you can totally relax the muscles of your neck while you plan your next move. It also allows for more body contact, which may help her feel connected.

Secret to success:

Your best stroke will be to use your tongue in a downward direction, taste bud-side up, over her clitoral hood.

Women who are more sensitive may prefer this downward stroke. Alternate this with a light upward stroke using the smoother underside of your tongue.

Rear approach

How it's done:

Tongue your partner from behind while she is on all fours.

Advantage:

Your access is somewhat limited, but she will be very exposed.

This approach also allows a strong downward stroke and it is ideal for kissing and sucking her vulva.

Secret to success:

For more exposure, have her lower her head onto the bed.

Over your shoulder

How it's done:

Get your partner to lie flat on her back and approach her vagina from between her legs. Have her place one leg over your shoulder and leave the other leg flat on the bed, under your shoulder and arm.

She should twist her hips slightly, elevating the hip on the side of the raised leg.

(You can help by supporting her raised hip with your other arm.)

Advantage:

This position is ideal for women who are particularly sensitive along one side of the clitoris.

Secret to success:

With one hip raised, she is able to add some movement to aid in your stroking or to help move you to the perfect spot. Encourage her to wriggle a little to help get it right.

The hovering butterfly

How it's done:

Lie on your back with your partner straddling you, facing towards the headboard and bracing herself against the wall.

Advantage:

This position is a favorite of many women, and it is a good one to use as your partner nears orgasm.

She'll be able to control your speed, pressure, and the angle of her pelvis to allow you access to specific areas.

With her partner somewhat hidden beneath her, she can easily drift off into her own world, which may help her climax.

Secret to success:

Let her call the shots – don't follow her if she lifts her pelvis off your mouth and don't try to reach for spots she's pulled out of the target zone.
Work with what's right in front of you.
The stronger tongue stroke here is upward.

Stand and Deliver

How it's done:

She stands. You kneel down in front of her.

Have her put a leg over one of your shoulders, and help her keep her balance by placing an arm around her opposite thigh to support the small of her back with your hand.

Advantage:

This is a great first position to use as you're undressing, or in the shower.

Secret to success:

Since her legs are not very open, there's less opportunity for direct clitoral stimulation, so use a hand to gently hold her open – or have her hold herself open for better access.

Chair therapy

How it's done:

Have your partner sit on a chair with her legs wide open. You take it from there.

Advantage:

This is a good position for either beginning the slow build-up with loose, broad, open strokes, or at the end with stronger suction moves.

Your partner is able to easily guide you, and she is able to get a full view of you between her legs, which is a turn-on for many women.

Secret of success:

Access:
Make sure the chair you use gives you plenty of clearance to move around.

Or add an extra kick to proceedings by using a swivel chair where you can direct her movements.

10 Worst Cunnilingus Mistakes

1 Making like a gynecologist

Sure, you're curious about what a pussy looks like up close. Go ahead and take a good look. But don't spread her labia open so wide that she feels like she's getting her annual pelvic exam at the gynecologist. Just use your fingertips to gently hold back her lips and slip your tongue in there.

2 The head shake

Don't emulate the exaggerated oral techniques in porn movies, especially that move where the guy sticks his tongue straight out and instead of licking, shakes his whole head side to side between the woman's legs till his ears slap against her thighs. It looks dumb even on camera and it doesn't work in real life.

3 Blowing air up her coochie

Do not form a seal around her vagina with your lips and blow into it. What, do you think she's a blow-up doll? Blowing lightly or breathing on and around the pussy is hot, but blowing air into the vagina is just dangerous and can lead to serious queefing (pussy farts).

4 Lapping like a dog

It's good to lick, and it's good to keep your tongue loose and relaxed. But don't get sloppy or slobbery. Use a little restraint and don't pant. If you're oral technique reminds her of her pet Golden Retriever, that won't be a turn-on.

5 Clit hickeys

Hickeys are so high school, but if you want leave your mark, do it on her neck, arm, tit or thigh. Don't clamp your mouth around her clit and suck it so hard you give her a welt. Strong suction on the clit (sucking it like a vacuum cleaner) isn't going to feel very good to her and might hurt.

6 Drunken pussy eating

This is as bad as a drunken blowjob, and you'll really ruin the moment if you're so wasted that you toss your cookies in her crotch. Remember, keggers and cunnilingus do not mix. To do a good job eating her out, you need to be able to pay attention and coordinate your tongue action. If you don't throw up, you still might pass out, and that pretty much guarantees you won't get another date with her.

7 Singing the Alphabet Song

Some guys like to use the trick of spelling the letters of the alphabet on her clit using their tongue. Fine, just don't start singing "Now I know my ABCs" while you're doing it. If you're going to get studious while you're down in her muff, try composing your term paper with your tongue. It may be the first time anybody ever got off on Kafka.

8 Jabbing and stabbing

Having someone insistently jabbing and poking their pointy tongue on your clit and into your pussy is just as creepy and uncomfortable in oral sex as it is in French kissing. It makes you come off as overeager and unskilled. Relax your tongue and take your time. Gently caress her clit and let her bring her pubes to you.

9 Orthodontia and pubes don't mix

Some of you may still be wearing braces. If so, make sure she shaves or at least trims or you're going to end up snagged in her short curlies. It'll be extremely painful for her and gross for you when you have to pick the hairs out of your teeth. Of course, the worst is if you're cheating on your girlfriend and she spots someone else's pubes in your teeth.

10 Blowing raspberries

It's fine to make some noise while eating pussy. Moaning is OK; most women like that. Even slurping is acceptable within limits. But sticking your face up in her bush and blowing raspberries or making fart sounds is not going to go over well. Neither will burp.

More Tips to Please Her & Cunnilingus Curious Facts

KISS FIRST. Avoiding her lips and diving straight for the erogenous zones makes her feel like you're paying by the hour and trying to get your money's worth by cutting out non-essentials. A properly passionate kiss is the ultimate form of foreplay.

DON'T BLOW TOO HARD IN HER EAR. Admit it, some kid at school told you girls love this. Well, there's a difference between being erotic and blowing as if you're trying to extinguish the candles on your 50th birthday cake. That hurts.

SHAVE. You often forget you have a porcupine strapped to your chin which you rake repeatedly across your partner's face and thighs. When she turns her head from side to side, it's not passion, it's avoidance.

ABOUT SQUEEZING HER BREAST. Most men act like a housewife testing a melon for ripeness when they get their hand on a pair. Stroke, caress, and smooth them.

ABOUT BITING HER NIPPLES. Why do men fasten onto a woman's nipples, and then clamp down like they're trying to deflate her body via her breasts? Nipples are highly sensitive. They can't stand up to chewing. Lick and suck them gently. Flicking your tongue across them is good. Pretending they're a doggie toy isn't good.

ABOUT TWIDDLING HER NIPPLES. Stop doing that thing where you twiddle the nipples between fingers and thumb like you're trying to find a radio station in a hilly area. Focus on the whole breasts, not just the exclamation points.

DON'T IGNORE THE OTHER PARTS OF HER BODY. A woman is not a highway with just three turn-offs: Breast-vile East and West, and the Mid-town Tunnel. There are vast areas of her body which you've ignored far too often as you go bombing straight into downtown Vagina. So start paying them some attention.

DON'T GET THE HAND TRAPPED. Poor manual dexterity in the underskirt region can result in tangled fingers and underpants. If you're going to be that aggressive, just ask her to take the damn things off.

DON'T LEAVE HER A LITTLE PRESENT. Condom disposal is the man's responsibility. You wore it, you store it.

DON'T ATTACK THE CLITORIS. Direct pressure is very unpleasant, so gently rotate your fingers along side of the clitoris.

DON'T STOP FOR A BREAK. Women, unlike men, don't pick up where they left off. If you stop, they plummet back to square one very fast. If you can tell she's not there, keep going at all costs, numb jaw or not.

The Masters Guide to Cunnilingus

DON'T UNDRESS HER AWKWARDLY. Women hate looking stupid, but stupid she will look when naked at the waist with a sweater stuck over her head. Unwrap her like an elegant present, not a kid's toy.

DON'T GIVE HER A WEDGIE DURING FOREPLAY. Stroking her gently through her panties can be very sexy. Pulling the material up between her thighs and yanking it back and forth is not.

DON'T BE OBSESSED WITH THE VAGINA. Although most men can find the clitoris without maps, they still believe that the vagina is where it's all at. No sooner is your hand down there than you're trying to stuff stolen bank notes up a chimney. This is okay in principle, but if you're not careful, it can hurt - so don't get carried away. It's best to pay more attention to her clitoris and the exterior of her vagina at first, then gently slip a finger inside her and see if she likes it.

DON'T MASSAGE TOO ROUGHLY. You're attempting to give her a sensual, relaxing massage to get her in the mood. Hands and fingertips are okay; elbows and knees are not.

DON'T UNDRESS PREMATURELY. Don't force the issue by stripping before she's at least made some move toward getting your stuff off, even if it's just undoing a couple of buttons.

DON'T TAKE YOUR PANTS OFF FIRST. A man in socks and underpants is at his worst. Lose the socks fist.

DON'T GO TOO FAST. When you get to the penis-in-vagina situation, the worst thing you can do is pump away like an industrial power tool - she'll soon feel like an assembly-line worker made obsolete by your technology. Build up slowly, with clean, straight, regular thrusts.

DON'T GO TOO HARD. If you bash your great triangular hip bones into her thigh or stomach, the pain is equal to two weeks of horseback riding concentrated into a few seconds.

DON'T COME TOO SOON. Every man's fear. With reason. If you shoot before you see the whites of her eyes, make sure you have a backup plan to ensure her pleasure too.

COME SOON ENOUGH. It may appear to you that humping for an hour without climaxing is the mark of a sex god, but to her it's more likely the mark of a numb vagina. At least buy some intriguing wall hangings, so she has something to hold her interest while you're playing Marathon Man.

DON'T ASK IF SHE HAS COME. Equate this with her asking: "Is it in?" You usually will be able to tell. Most women make noise. But if you really don't know, don't ask right there on the spot, the first time. Bring it up later, as part of your normal couple communication.

DON'T PERFORM ORAL SEX TOO GENTLY. Don't act like a giant cat at a saucer of milk. Get your whole mouth down there, and concentrate on gently rotating or flicking your tongue on her clitoris.

DON'T NUDGE HER HEAD DOWN. Men persist in doing this until she's eyeball-to-penis, hoping that it will lead very swiftly to mouth-to-penis. All women hate this. It's about three steps from being dragged to a cave by their hair. If you want her to use her mouth, use yours; try talking seductively to her.

WARN HER BEFORE YOU CLIMAX. Sperm tastes like sea water mixed with egg white. Not everybody likes it. When she's performing oral sex, warn her before you come so she can do what's necessary.

The Masters Guide to Cunnilingus

DON'T MOVE AROUND DURING FELLATIO. Don't thrust. She'll do all the moving during fellatio. You just lie there. And don't grab her head.

ABOUT PENIS HYGIENE. Boys should be taught how to wash daily underneath the penis foreskin. If your parents "forgot" about it, you may be sexually challenged by an awkwardly foul-smelling penis. Worry no more! Get in the shower and follow these instructions:
- Gently pull the foreskin back away from the head of the penis;
- Rinse the head of the penis and inside fold of the foreskin with soap and warm water;
- Use your finger to remove any deposits from the fold;
- Pull the foreskin back over the head of the penis.

DON'T TAKE ETIQUETTE ADVICE FROM PORN MOVIES. In X-rated movies, women seem to love it when men ejaculate over them. In real life, it just means more laundry to do.

DON'T MAKE HER RIDE ON TOP FOR AGES. Asking her to be on top is fine. Lying there grunting while she does all the hard work is not. Caress her gently, so that she doesn't feel quite so much like the captain of a schooner. And let her have a rest.

DON'T ATTEMPT ANAL SEX AND PRETEND IT WAS AN ACCIDENT. This is how men earn a reputation for not being able to follow directions. If you want to put it there, ask her first. And don't think that being drunk is an excuse.

ABOUT TAKING PICTURES. When a man says "Can I take a photo of you?" she'll hear the words "...to show my buddies." At least let her have custody of them.

BE IMAGINATIVE ENOUGH. Imagination is anything from drawing patterns on her back to pouring honey on her and licking it off. Fruit, vegetables, ice and feathers are all handy props; a bath or shower with a richly perfumed soap won't be forgotten; hot candle wax and permanent dye are a no no.

DON'T SLAP YOUR STOMACH AGAINST HERS. There is no less erotic noise. It's as sexy as a belching contest.

DON'T ARRANGE HER IN STUPID POSES. If she wants to do advanced yoga in bed, fine, but unless she's a Romanian gymnast, don't get too ambitious. Ask yourself if you want a sexual partner with snapped hamstrings.

DON'T LOOK FOR HER PROSTATE. Read this carefully: Anal stimulation feels good for men because they have a prostate. Women don't have one. Some women do enjoy anal sex. Just don't take it for granted.

DON'T GIVE LOVE BITES. It is highly erotic to exert some gentle suction on the sides of the neck, if you do it carefully. No woman wants to have to wear turtlenecks and jaunty scarves for weeks on end.

DON'T BARK INSTRUCTIONS. Don't shout encouragement like a coach with a megaphone. It's not a big turn-on.

ABOUT TALKING DIRTY. It makes you sound like a lonely magazine editor calling a 1-900 line. If she likes nasty talk, she'll let you know.

DO CARE ABOUT WHETHER SHE COMES. You have to finish the job. Keep on trying until you get it right, and she might even do the same for you.

DON'T SQUASH HER. Men generally weigh more than women, so if you lay on her a bit too heavily, she will turn blue.

DON'T THANK HER. Never thank a woman for having sex with you. Your bedroom is not a soup kitchen. If you really want to show her how meaningful she is to you, try kissing her tenderly, all over, instead of falling asleep like a bear.

And a bonus tip:

LOCATION, LOCATION, LOCATION. Don't let routine settle in. Try new and "forbidden" locations: A woodsy area (don't forget the bug spray); your backyard (in the middle of the night); your car or better yet, your van (remember those days); even on a boat (anchored offshore). It will provide that *"don't get caught"* excitement that might be lacking after a while in the plain safety of your old bedroom.

Facts on Oral Sex

- Oral sex was illegal in Georgia until 1998.
- There is an alcoholic cocktail named the "Cunnilingus."
- The Chinese Empress Wu Hu demanded visiting ignitaries to lick her clit before any discussion took place.
- The Jehovah's Witnesses say any form of oral sex is "against nature" and therefore sinful.

KAMASUTRA AFTER ORAL SEX

Basic positions:

The union of the bee

The woman sits on the penis of her partner, himself seated with his legs outstretched. She can then move up and down while resting on her hands and legs. He lifts her buttocks or thighs to accompany her movements.

Variant: The man can lean against a wall for support. The woman can kneel down instead of sitting, so that she can lean forward more easily and change the angle of penetration into her vagina.

Plusses
- The woman has better control of the depth of penetration than with other from behind positions.
- The vagina's front wall and the G-spot are well stimulated.
- In this passive position, the man can more easily caress

his partner's breasts and clitoris.

Minuses
- Tiring position for the man if he has no support.

Andromaches's position

The man is lying on his back. His partner places herself above him, crouching or kneeling, keeping her torso straight up. She perfectly controls the depth and the rhythm of penetration and can give a free rein to her fantasies of domination.

Plusses
- The woman retains total control enabling her to be more confident and to find the right motions to maximize her pleasure.
- The man has his hands free to give his partner even more pleasure by caressing her breasts, her buttocks or her clitoris.
- This position procures a good stimulation of the G-spot.

Minuses
- The angle of penetration is sometimes uncomfortable for the man, or even painful if his penis bends.

The balanced position

The man sits on a chair or on the edge of the bed. The woman turns her back to him and sits on his thighs. Once he has penetrated her, she can lean down and make her vagina go back and forth on his penis. To better stabilize her position, she can hold his knees and he can hold her by the breasts.

Plusses
- Position allowing rather deep penetration with a good amplitude of motion.
- The man can easily stimulate his partner's breasts and clitoris with his hands to better lead her to orgasm.

Minuses
- Not always easy to keep the balance.

The position of the rider

The man lies on his back and the woman, fronting him, kneels above him with her thighs around his. She completely controls the depth of penetration and the movements. She moves horizontally as well as vertically to maximize the stimulation of her clitoris and of the walls of her vagina, or to bring her partner to an orgasm.

Plusses
- The woman has more freedom and is more active : she chooses the type, the speed and the rhythm of the motions.
- The man remains more passive and can concentrate on his sensations and pleasure, while caressing his partner's back.

Minuses
- Lack of originality ? You can always use a variant or try another position after a while.

The union of the tiger

Starting from the Missionary Position, the woman lifts her legs to her torso. She can adjust the depth of penetration and the sensations by varying the angle of her legs. She may also take hold of her partner's buttocks and press them to her to augment the depth of penetration.

Plusses
- By lifting her legs, the woman favors deeper penetration and can at least partly control her sensations.
- The man's pelvic bone brushes against his partner's

The Masters Guide to Cunnilingus

vulva and stimulates her clitoris.

Minuses
- This position requires a good elasticity of the woman, particularly if she draws her legs very close to her torso.

The Perfect Alignment Position

The woman lays on top of the man with her legs open to facilitate penetration. Once the penis is well in place, both straighten their legs so that the two lovers are superimposed in a perfect alignment. The woman can then start the stimulation by rubbing her body laterally and horizontally against her partner's.

Plusses
- Very intimate position offering maximum contact between the 2 partners.
- The tightened vagina walls procure more intense sensations.
- Recommended for tantric sex.

Minuses
- The depth of penetration and the amplitude of movement are both limited.

The Union of the Antelope

Kneeling on the ground, the woman holds the edge of the bed and straightens her back. The man kneels down and penetrates her from behind

Variant: the woman can open her legs wide on either side of her partner's to offer him a maximum opening, or she can tighten her thighs to compress her vagina and squeeze her partner's penis.

Plusses
- Good stimulation of the vagina's forward wall and of the G-Spot.
- The man can easily stimulate his partner's clitoris and breasts with his hands.
- The woman can easily fantasize about imaginary partners.

Minuses
- Beware of scraping your knees on the ground unless you have a thick carpet.

The Position of the Swing

The man lies on his back. The woman turns her back on him and crouches down on his penis, supporting herself on her feet. Or she kneels down with her legs on either side of her partner's hips, for a greater amplitude of motion.

Plusses
- This position offers the man an exceptional view of his partner's behind, and of the penetration.
- It allows a good amplitude of motion, particularly with the woman kneeling down, to procure maximum pleasure to the man and lead him rapidly to orgasm.
- It lets the woman easily fantasize about imaginary partners.

Minuses
- The angle of penetration can make the position uncomfortable for some men.

The Missionary Position

It is the best known position, universally appreciated by both novices and experts. The woman is lying on her back and the man lies between her legs to penetrate her.

Variant : A few cushions placed under the woman's buttocks change the penetration angle and allow a deeper penetration.

Plusses
- Natural and comfortable position for both partners.
- Good freedom of movement for the man.
- The couple can look at each other, or kiss. Their hands are free for lots of other stimulations.

Minuses
- The woman's freedom of movement is quite limited.
- The position can become tedious, requiring a change : one should not abuse of it!

The Union of the Cow (or the Doggie-Style Position)

A classic position, universally appreciated for the excitation and the intense sensations it gives to both partners. The woman is on all fours. The man, kneeling, penetrates her from behind.
Variant : The woman may make the position even more comfortable with a few cushions under her elbows.

Plusses
- Very good stimulation of the vagina's forward wall and G-Spot.
- Very lively and deep penetration.
- The man can easily stimulate his partner's breasts and clitoris with his hands.
- Very exciting view for the man, allowing him to indulge in his domination fantasies.
- The woman can easily fantasize about imaginary partners.

Minuses
- Some women may feel humiliated by this position.
- The position can be painful for the woman if the penis bumps into her vagina's bottom.

Intermediary Positions

The Union of the Eagle
Laying on their side, the two lovers enlace themselves with their arms and legs, the woman wrapping her legs around her partner's waist. The man bends his legs slightly to facilitate penetration.

Plusses
- Very intimate position allowing maximum contact between the two partners.
- Good penetration depth when the man bends his thighs between his partner's.

Minuses
- Limited amplitude of movement..

The Fruit Position

A variant of the Indra position : procuring similar sensations but reducing the woman's crushing feeling when her partner is on top. She keeps one leg against his torso and frees her other leg to the side.

Plusses
- Deep penetration.
- Strong stimulation of the vagina thanks to its compression.

Minuses
- Could be painful if the penis bumps into the vagina's bottom.

The Courtesan Position

The woman is seated on a chair or on the edge of the bed. The man kneels down to penetrate her. She then wraps her legs around him.

Variant : the woman can sit on a table or a desk, so that the man can remain standing.

Plusses
- Comfortable position for the two partners.
- Allows good amplitude of motions and good depth of penetration.
- Can easily be practiced outside the bedroom.

Minuses
- The feasibility of the position is very dependent on the height of the woman's support.

The Dance of the Missionary

Starting from the Missionary position and penetration, the woman squeezes her buttocks and arches her back, then undulates her behind in circular lateral and vertical motions.

Plusses
- Very good stimulation for the man, favoring a rapid orgasm.

Minuses
- Difficult to do for long : tiring for both partners.

The Union of the Emu

Both partners are standing, and she turns her back to him. The man attracts his partner to him and penetrates her from behind. She leans forward to modify the angle of penetration and make it deeper.

*Variant*s : the woman holds herself with her hands against a wall or a window ; or she can rest her chest on a table or a desk. She can then loosen up more easily and her partner can penetrate her more vigorously.

Plusses
- A very exciting position allowing the man to fulfill his

domination fantasies,... and allowing the woman to easily fantasize about imaginary partners.
- Deep penetration procuring very good stimulation of the woman's vaginal walls and of her G-Spot.
- The man can also simultaneously caress his partner's clitoris or breasts.

Minuses
- A difficult position when the two partners are of very different heights. But the man can either bend his knees or step on a support to make it easier.

The Union of the Oyster

The woman lies on her back and folds her thighs to her belly. The man holds her by the knees and penetrates her. He uses her thighs as a support to facilitate his back and forth motions and to maintain the proper rhythm.

Plusses
- The position allows deep penetration and good amplitude of motions.
- The woman's vagina is compressed around the man's penis, for a good stimulation of both partners.

Minuses
- This position may inflict pain to the woman if the penetration is too deep or too vigorous.

The Union of the Octopus

Lying on her back with the man between her legs, the woman lifts her thighs and bottom over his knees and thighs. He lifts her by the hips to change the angle and the depth of penetration.

The Masters Guide to Cunnilingus

Plusses
- Comfortable position for both partners.
- Deep penetration.
- The man can free one hand to caress the breasts of his partner.

Minuses
- The amplitude of movement is limited.

The Union of the Turtle

Starting from the Position of the Perfect Alignment, the man opens his legs to let his partner's thighs slide between his.

Plusses
- Very intimate position maximizing the contact between the two partners.
- Procures more intense sensations as the vagina closes itself of the penis.

Minuses
- The penetration is not as deep as when the woman keeps her legs open.
- The amplitude of movement is more limited.

The Union of the Lovers

Both partners standing face to face, the man rubs his penis against her partner's vulva. After a few minutes of rubbing, the vulva opens naturally to allow shallow penetration. If the woman is shorter than the man, she can wear high heels or step on a support (such as a telephone directory under each foot) to reach the appropriate height.

Plusses
- A practical position for impromptu sex in all situations.
- Good stimulation of both the clitoris and the glans.

The Position of the Plough

The woman is lying on her back with her behind at the edge of the bed. The man kneels down between her legs, she wraps them around him and he penetrates her, keeping his penis horizontal.

Variant : The man can remain standing if his partner lies down on a table or a desk.

Plusses
- The horizontal alignment of the penis and the vagina procure new sensations.
- This position allows deep penetration and good stimulation of the vagina's walls.
- This position is exciting, particularly in the standing mode and in a locale different from the bedroom.

Minuses
- The feasibility and comfort of this position are very dependent on the height of the bed or of the table.

The Posture of the Spoons

The woman lies on her side, with her legs in the foetal position. The man places himself behind and marries the contours of his partner to penetrate her. The man then has free hands to caress her breats and clitoris, while at the same time being able to kiss the nape of her neck and behind her ears.

Plusses
- Soft and relaxing position favoring caresses and the intimacy of the couple.
- The woman can easily masturbate herself or guide her partner's hand to reach an orgasm more rapidly.

Minuses
- The amplitude of movements is limited.

The Union of the Goddess

The man is sitting on the bed, and can have his back against the wall for a better hold. Fronting him, the woman sits on his penis and guides it into her vagina. She wraps her legs around him, and she undulates her behind for a good stimulation of her clitoris and of the walls of her vagina.

Plusses
- Intimate position allowing the couple to kiss each other and the man to lick his partner's breasts.
- Deep penetration as well as good clitoris stimulation.
- Recommended to delay the orgasm of men who suffer from premature ejaculation.

Minuses
- Limited stimulation for the man.

The Anvil Position

Lying on her back, the woman places her feet on top of her partner's shoulders. This position favours a very deep position. It should be avoided unless the preliminaries have been sufficient to allow the woman's vagina to reach its full size and to be properly lubricated.

Plusses
- This position allows maximum penetration.
- It procures intense sensations to the woman, particularly when the man ejaculates in this position.
- It allows the man to fulfill his domination fantasies.

Minuses
- This position requires a very good suppleness of the woman.
- It could be painful to her if her vagina is not sufficiently lubricated, or if her partner's penis bangs into the rear wall of her vagina.

The Union of the Magpie

This position is a variant from the "Union of the Goddess", where the man sits on a chair rather than a bed. More stable and comfortable, this position allows the partners to move more easily. It can be the starting point of a sequence where this position is followed by the "Suspended Union", then the "Posture of the Pillar", to end with the "Missionary Position".

Plusses
- Very intimate and comfortable position for both partners.
- Allows a rather deep penetration and a good amplitude of vertical motions by the woman.
- Convenient to make love at work or in the lavatories of a public place.

Minuses
- The man's amplitude of movement is restricted.

The Posture of the Pillar

Both partners are kneeling on the bed. The woman slides her thighs over her partner's and guides his penis towards her vagina.

Plusses
- Very intimate position allowing each partner to kiss and caress the other comfortably.
- Recommended for Tantric Love.

Minuses
- The stimulation possibilities are limited and so is the depth of penetration.

Expert Positions

The Amazon Position

The man is seated on a chair. The woman sits Amazon-like on one of his thighs and guides his penis towards her vagina. Once the penis is introduced, she can contract her vagina muscles to keep it in and avoid unwanted withdrawals.

Plusses
- The man can easily caress the breasts and the clitoris of his partner to bring her to orgasm more easily.
- Position recommended for the man suffering from premature ejaculation.

Minuses
- Limited amplitude of movement and shallow penetration.

The Union of the Cat
Starting either from the missionary position or from the position of the Rider, both partners rock to the side, slowly to avoid unwanted withdrawal.

Plusses
- An intimate and soft position, allowing the two partners to look at each other and to kiss, while avoiding the feeling of domination for either partner.

Minuses
- The amplitude of movement and the depth of penetration are both limited.
- There is a risk of involuntary withdrawal during the rocking aside.

The Union of the Butterfly

Starting from a position where the woman is sitting on the man, facing him, she rocks backwards and brings her legs forward, while the man leans backwards and holds himself with his arms. Then both partners move their pelvis in a circular motion, but in opposite directions. The woman may also use her legs to initiate back and forth motions along her partner's penis.

Plusses
- Original and aesthetic position.
- The distance between the two partners' heads allows them to watch each other and observe their mutual reactions.
- A good variety of pelvis movements.

Minuses
- Rather athletic position, requiring practice.
- The hands of the two partners are tied up.

The Suspended Union

The couple is standing up face to face, the woman grips her partner's back, suspends herself, and firmly wraps her legs around the man's waist. He holds her by her buttocks and back and penetrates her. She may also lean her back against a wall for an easier hold.

Plusses
- Exciting position, achievable anywhere, in all situations.

Minuses
- Rather athletic position, hard to maintain unless the woman is very light.

Extreme Positions

The Bamboo Position

Starting from penetration in the missionary position, the woman slides one leg over her partner's shoulder while he brings up his knee. After a while, she brings down her leg and slides up the other one, both partners repeating the movement on the other side. Each movement is repeated several times.

Plusses
- A fun position, quite acrobatic : for the most daring.

Minuses
- Limited stimulation possibilities.
- Requires a great suppleness of the woman.

The Posture of the Star

The woman is lying on her back and opens her legs wide. The man places one leg between hers and penetrates his partner from the side, holding himself with his opposite arm. He can rub her clitoris with his thigh to increase the stimulation.

Plusses
- The penetration from the side procures new sensations to both partners.
- The woman's vulva and clitoris can be stimulated by the man rubbing them with his thigh.
- The two partners are free to kiss each other, and each partner has one hand free for caresses.

Minuses
- The motions of the man's pelvis are restricted.

The Indra Position

The man is on his knees and straightens his chest. The woman is lying in front of him, raises her legs, and puts her feet on his chest. As he penetrates her, the man leans forward to press his partner's thighs against her breasts.

Plusses
- Maximum, very deep penetration.
- Strong stimulation for the woman as her abdomen and vagina are compressed.

Minuses
- May be painful for the woman if her partner's penis comes against her vagina's back wall.

The Posture of the Moon

The woman is lying on her back. Starting from a kneeling position, the man brings one leg around, then the other, until he sits in front of the woman, still penetrating her. The two partners can embrace and continue the movements with simultaneous impulsions of their pelvis'.

Plusses
- A very original position allowing deep penetration.
- Good clitoris stimulation by the man's pelvis bone.

Minuses
- Requires a very good suppleness of the man.

The Posture of the Reed

The woman is lying on her back and the man kneels between her legs. As she holds herself with her feet and head, he takes hold of her hips and lifts them high up. She arches her back to align her vagina with his penis. He continues to hold her by the hips as he penetrates her vigorously, watching her reactions.

Plusses
- Exciting and provocative position allowing a deep and vigorous penetration, together with a good view of each partner by the other.

Minuses
- Requires a good flexibility of the woman's back.

The Posture of the Willow

The man kneels down and the woman, facing him, sits on his thighs keeping her torso straight. He penetrates her then leans far forward while holding her buttocks with one hand and her back with the other. The woman may support herself on one hand, to be able to undulate her pelvis up and down.

Plusses
- A good transitory position to go from sitting to lying down without withdrawing.

Minuses
- Athletic position for muscular men only, or if their partner is very light!

The Posture of the Stem

The man kneels in front of the woman, who is lying on her back. She raises her legs and puts one on her partner's shoulder and the other on his opposite forearm. He lifts her buttocks and penetrates her. To maximize the pleasure, she will keep her thighs as tight as she can, and he will alternate deep vigorous penetrations and softer shallow ones.
Variant : For lazy ones, a few cushions under the woman's buttocks will make the position easier to maintain.

Plusses
- Original position, exciting for both partners.
- The man keeps a good mobility of his pelvis allowing
- vigorous penetrations.

Minuses
- Rather athletic position requiring a good physical condition.

The Posture of the Scissors

Starting from Andromache's position, the woman topples backwards, with her head down to her partner's feet. This position is recommended to delay the man's ejaculation.

Plusses
- Allows a very good manual stimulation of the clitoris.
- Exciting view for the man.
- Good position to delay the man's orgasm.

Minuses
- Requires a very good suppleness of the woman.

The Posture of the Great Aperture

Starting from Andromache's Position, the woman rocks her back backwards and slowly slides one leg under one of her partner's. She takes care to hold her partner's penis well inserted and held in her vagina, avoiding unwanted withdrawal. She can then move her pelvis sideways, back and forth, to experiment with new sensations.

Plusses
- An original position, that can remain comfortable for both partners.
- The sideways penetration stimulates the walls of the woman's vagina and procures new sensations.

The Masters Guide to Cunnilingus

Minuses
- A risk of unwanted withdrawal during the rocking movement.
- The amplitude of the pelvis motions is somewhat restricted.

The Lotus Position

Lying on her back, the woman folds her legs in the lotus position, presenting her well opened vagina to her partner.

Plusses
- Amusing and original position.

Minuses
- Requires a good suppleness of the woman.
- Difficult to hold for long, and sometimes painful for the woman.

The Moving Windmill

This is a moving position whereby the woman rotates on her partner, using his penis as an axis.
Step one : The woman crouches down on her partner so that he penetrates her. She starts the stimulations with up and down movements on her partner's penis.
Step two : Still holding his penis within, she moves her left leg over to the right of his chest and starts pivoting.
Step three : the woman is now facing backwards, her back to her partner. She continues the vertical stimulations but leans forward to change the penetration angle. Then she resumes the rotation movement until she is facing her partner again...

Plusses
- Amusing and original position bringing many different sensations without interrupting the penetration.
- Recommended for Tantric Sex.

Minuses
- Important risk of unwanted withdrawal during steps 2 & 3.

The Moving Wheel

This position is performed in three steps, as the man must rotate very slowly on his partner, using his penis as the axis of rotation. The cycle may be repeated several times and is well suited to Tantric Sex.

First step : The two partners are in the classic Missionary Position. The man is between his partner's legs and penetrates her.

Second step: The man slides his left leg, then his right leg, over the woman's right leg. Then he rotates slowly around his penis.

Third step : After a 180° rotation, the man places his legs on either side of his partner's shoulders and kisses her feet. He then resumes his rotation until he has come back to his initial position.

Plusses
- Unusual and amusing position, bringing a diversity of sensations.
- Recommended for Tantric Love.

Minuses
- The possibilities of stimulations are quite restricted.
- Unwanted withdrawal is guaranteed with novices.

The Union of the Monkey

The man is lying on his back, with his legs straight up. The woman sits on the top of his thighs, using his feet as a backrest. The two partners hold themselves by the wrists, to maintain a stable position. He then lifts her with his feet, to start an up and down stimulation. The woman adds to this stimulation by undulating her pelvis in a lateral circular motion.

Plusses
- Original and fun position for creative couples.

Minuses
- A difficult to control position.
- The man may feel crushed by his partner.

The Ying and the Yang Position

The man crouches on a stable and solid surface, and the woman, facing him, sits on his knees. For better stability, the man may lean his back on the edge of the bed or a similar low support.

Plusses
- Original and fun position.

Minuses
- Difficult position to maintain without a support, requiring good balance and good muscular power of the man.

Fantasies and Practices

Understand your fantasies and learn about those of others..

What is Sadomasochism?

1. Origin and Definition of Sadomasochism

   Richard von Krafft-Ebing, a neurologist and psychologist, borrowed the names of two famous 18th-19th century French and Austrian authors, Sade and Sacher-Masoch, to name a sexual perversion which he called Sadomasochism. In this combination of sadism and masochism, sexual pleasure is obtained through both causing and receiving physical pain and humiliation. According to Freud, it is the most frequent and important form of perversion. Sadism involves obtaining sexual gratification by inflicting physical or psychological suffering on others. Masochism involves obtaining sexual gratification through having someone else inflict physical or psychological suffering to oneself. The practice of sadomasochism is only considered a pathological deviance when it is the only means by which a person can achieve sexual arousal.

A perversion or a game ?

S&M can be a liberating way of acting out deeply-felt desires. It can also be just a form of role-play used to add a little spice to normal sexual pleasures. In a few cases, sadomasochism can also be a real perversion with serious consequences for those involved.

The perversion :

It classed as a perversion, or a pathological substitute for normal sexual intercourse, when it is the only means through which someone can relieve particularly deep and persistent sex drives. It is generally not considered a crime when it takes place between two consenting adults, but laws of course prohibit acts of torture or cruelty. Clearly sadomasochism inflicted to a child or to a non-consenting adult may be considered an act of torture and cruelty under most countries' laws.

The game :

Many couples in fact like to play erotic games of domination/submission. These can be defined as games played between two adult partners respecting each other as equals. This implies that both partners consent, and just want to experiment. Under these conditions, the game is played to intensify mutual emotions and sensations. It is often also a means of more easily satisfying one's sexual desires. When controlled, and where the liberty and integrity of each partner are respected, sadomasochistic game may indeed relieve certain sexual tensions or anxieties. Various games are played :

In games where one partner dominates and the other submits, this is termed domination/submission. Such scenarios usually involve one partner seducing, exciting, and/or frustrating the other, and in the end satisfying them. Games involving some sort of punishment are called submission/discipline games.

So called S.M. (Sadomasochistic) games generally imply the use of whips, straps, swatters or other accessories to inflict various degrees of pain. This pain, real or feigned, becomes a source of pleasure and intense stimulation.These types of relationships are above all intellectual in nature. Domination is a power game, a game of erotic strength, a cerebral sport. Its foremost aspect is the intellectual, often more important than the physical aspect of sex. But it is also a seduction game : the master, with the display of his or her power, seduces the slave, who seduces the master by willingly serving him or her. In such games of powerful erotic content, sexual intercourse is not an end in itself.

Homosexuality

Homosexuality is when an individual feels sexual desire for another person of the same sex. It is a fluid concept as it can be a temporary or permanent phenomenon.

Statistics on homosexuality

It is difficult to find statistics on homosexuality, as for a long time it was considered taboo and many homosexuals did not admit their sexual preferences. However, the Kinsey study of the US population in the 60s showed that 37% of male respondents had had homosexual experiences, while 5% were exclusively homosexual. 15% of women had had lesbian experiences, but only 1% to 3% were exclusively homosexual.

The causes of homosexuality

There has been a lot of debate about the "causes" of homosexuality. It may be psychological and/or genetic. It was thought that psychological factors could cause a predisposition to homosexuality. Various people have put forward "explanations" of varying credibility, such as problematic relationships with parents, non-judgmental education, insecurity about sexual identity, a traumatic childhood, a precocious interest in sex, pre-adolescent masturbatory fantasies, or even peer pressure. However, it is possible to have all these experiences without becoming homosexual.

In recent years, genetic research has put forward the possibility of genetic causes, or even of a "homosexual gene". In one of these studies, Dr. Michael Bailey of Northwestern University studied 110 pairs of identical twins who were separated at birth and grew up in different environments. The results showed that if one of the twins was homosexual, there was a 52% chance that the other one would be too.

Male homosexuality

A distinction is made between the active partner (who does the penetrating) and the passive partner (who is penetrated). These roles can be interchangeable. Many homosexuals say they have always been attracted to men, ever since puberty. Masculine homosexuality can also become manifest in later life. Some surveys have concluded that the mother, much more than the father, plays an important role in the development of male homosexuality.

Female homosexuality

Lesbians can be either "butch" (adopting a more masculine look) or "femme" (more feminine). Many homosexuals say they have always been attracted to women, since their youth. Apparently, the family environment has little effect on the development of female homosexuality, but certain events or situations may trigger it.

Eonism, better known as *transvestism*, derives its name from the chevalier d' Eon, a French adventurer at the court of king Louis XV in the 18th century, who was known for wearing women's clothes. It refers to a person's desire to wear the clothes of the opposite sex, sometimes in order to feel as if they belong to that sex. A transvestite may also move and act like a person of the opposite sex, in order to identify completely with it. This may be an occasional game or a real fetish. Transvestites may be homosexual, but they can just as easily be heterosexual.

Transvestism has recently come into fashion with the drag queen phenomenon, which has brought this fetish into the spotlight.

Transsexuality

Some people feel that their real self is a different gender to that of their bodies. They feel as though they "should" have been born as boys/girls and feel as if they are the victims of a mistake on the part of nature, which prevented them from being born as the opposite sex. They may therefore wish to try and become the man/woman that they want to be. This phenomenon generally dates back to childhood. It is known as transsexuality. These people are profoundly uncomfortable with their male/female bodies, feeling that they are foreign to them and out of kilter with their personalities.

Therefore, some men and women decide to take hormones or undergo surgery in order to develop the body which corresponds to their personality, with the external sexual characteristics of which they were deprived at birth. However, it is currently impossible to change sex completely. A man who has had his penis replaced with a vagina can look like a woman, but obviously cannot reproduce. Some countries such as the UK, Sweden and Denmark allow transsexuals to alter their legal status by changing the sex listed on their birth certificates, on production of the medical certificate for the surgery.

The Basis of a Sado-masochistic Relationship

1. What are sado-masochistic practices?

SM games can be played in different ways: the sexual aspect may be strongly present or completely absent. The practices are quite varied, from light to severe bondage, from spanking to humiliation or scarification. The domination may be physical or mental.So there is soft SM and hard SM. Some people go to extremes such as scatology, branding, scarification or infibulation. Our purpose here is not to describe such extremes, but rather to stay within the limits of harmless games.

In SM games, pain is often considered to be a sensation that is just as interesting to explore as any other. When a person is sexually aroused, his or her pain threshold, whether physical or psychological, is higher, and the pain felt may be transformed into pleasure. However, pain is not obligatory, just a possible option. It is a symbol of submission. The starting point is the desire to submit unconditionally. But submission without pain may just as easily create a state of euphoria, by triggering the production of endorphins.

The context:

Sado-masochistic games are often played as a ritual, in a pre-arranged scene, and using various accessories: boots, ropes, chains, handcuffs, leather, fur, latex, PVC, whips... In the scene, demands or orders are given, and if the rules are transgressed, the submissive partner is punished severely: spanking, flagellation with a whip or crop, piercing, scratching, burning, and so on.

Different sensations:

Strong sensations can be obtained by playing with heat, cold, or pinching. Wax, ice cubes and pincers can be used to achieve this. The triggering of adrenaline caused by these games excites both the slave and the master/mistress. Pincers are sometimes applied to the genitals or to the breasts of the designated victim. The sensation of pain often comes when the pincers are removed, but it may be relieved by gently pinching the affected flesh with the fingers. If you are using pincers for the first time, let your partner do it her- or himself, to reduce the possible fear. Be very careful with sensitive body areas if you use ice or hot wax.

Bondage:

In SM games, bondage involves tying up the submissive partner with ropes, chains, handcuffs, or simply a blindfold, to restrict their movements.

A blindfold can create a sense of mystery. If you can't see, you don't know what is going to happen, but you also feel as though you cannot be seen. When your hands are tied, you feel imprisoned, which some people find a relief. It is up to your partner to invent the game and you are subject to their desire. Being tied up can sometimes help you to relax, and it may even produce an enjoyable hypnotic state. Also, you can come without feeling guilty, since it is your partner who is in control the situation. So, paradoxically, being tied up procures a sort of freedom. Meanwhile, your partner may be very excited by the sight of you tied up and helpless. Be careful never to tie your partner's bonds too tightly. And never leave your partner alone. If tied up or gagged, your partner may be helpless in case of an unexpected problem, such as a fire. The master or mistress is responsible for the safety of the slave: he or she must evaluate all the parameters of the game to avoid accidents.

Corporal punishment:

Whips, floggers, paddles, crops and bunches of nettles can have strong erotic power when used for punishment. Flagellation is a very ancient sexual practice and is present in numerous erotic writings, including the Kama Sutra. The pain awakens the senses and concentrates the attention on a particular body area. Spanking is given with bare hands. The sound and the rhythm contribute to the pleasure of those for whom corporal punishment is an indispensable prelude to sexual intercourse, or a substitute for it. This practice may be reminiscent of childhood punishments and of the accompanying feelings of prudishness and shame. Spanking sessions may satisfy a whole variety of buried and repressed tendencies.

Speech:

In most cases, these practices are accompanied by verbal sado-masochism in the form of orders and/or insults. Keep in mind that this is a game, not the tortures of the Spanish Inquisition. The pain inflicted must remain under control. Contrasting gestures, such as caresses, can play down the intensity and help avoid real psychological harm. They can also help maintain sexual awareness and desire.

2. Online/offline meetings

The above practices are most often used within an established couple. However, single people are sometimes tempted by these games and search for a partner through want ads or the net. Finding a suitable partner is no easy task. For those who want to try, some advice may be useful in order to limit the risks inherent in such experiments:

Online:

Take your time. Don't suggest a meeting too fast. It is never a good idea to rush into a meeting. Learn about the person before giving your real name, address, or phone number. Be honest in describing the type of relationship you are looking for: tell the other party about your level of experience with SM practices, state your limits and ask about their experience and limits. Try to assess if their desires are compatible with your own.

First offline encounter:

Arrange the first meeting in a public place. Follow your instinct and do not forget that you are free to leave. A classic and very effective precaution: let a friend know what you are doing ahead of time; give as many details as possible on the person you are about to meet, as well as when and where.

Plan to call your friend to indicate all is well, or to use a code meaning you need help, and call discreetly once you have assessed the situation. Be patient. Avoid SM role-playing or having sex the first time you meet.

The first scene:

If you wish to continue the relationship, you should indicate your limits very clearly before the first SM scene, and learn about your partner's limits. Be exhaustive and ask for the same: you have no idea of the extent of your partner's imagination at this stage. Do not forget the classic precaution: your friend who knows of the encounter (not all the details, but at least when, where and phone number). If the meeting is at your place, do not unhook the phone. This meeting is still exploratory and must stay very soft. Get into it gradually, avoid being tied up, avoid excessive pain and extreme practices.

If the relationship is still to your liking, let it evolve... But be careful: accidents can happen very quickly. Keep emergency numbers and an extra set of keys for the handcuffs nearby...

Practicing Sado-masochis

1. Essential conditions for a happy and healthy SM relationship

No two sado-masochistic relationships are never completely identical, but some basic rules must always be respected. SM relationships between two partners must remain a game for both: they must be kept within certain limits. The following rules should allow couples to stay within these limits.

Trust:

SM activities should allow the couple to build and maintain a strong relationship based on the knowledge of each other and of each other's limits. A couple who experiment with SM games are often very close and like to communicate and share experiences. They also want to test their limits. Good communication between the dominant partner and the submissive one is indispensable for the success of the relationship. The submissive partner must talk about their feelings before and after the SM activities, and the dominant partner must be a good listener. The dom(me) must also be able to read the non-verbal signs given by the sub. Each must always know where the other's limits are and how far the game may be taken. Such in-depth understanding enhances the relationship. Because of the intimate knowledge required of one another, it is often difficult to engage in SM games with strangers. This is why even in SM clubs, these games are often practiced only between the two members of established couples.

Negotiation and respecting limits:

The dominant partner must know the sexual practices, fantasies, limits and taboos of the submissive partner. There must be proper discussion and negotiation on what each partner does and does not want. These limits vary between couples and may also evolve during their relationships. However, they should not be changed without prior agreement. These limits are the frontiers of the relationship, beyond which it could cease to exist.

In the last scene of the famous Adrian Lyne movie, "Nine and a half weeks", the dominant partner introduces a third person into the couple and breaks the bond linking him to his partner, which announces the end of the relationship. This illustrates the point of no return reached by trespassing one of the partner's limits in the SM game.

You have the right for your limits to be respected, but you must verbalise them, because by failing to speak you are tacitly consenting. If your partner does not respect your limits, you should seriously question the validity of the trust you have put in them. Also, telling your partner about your sexual fantasies does not necessarily mean that you want to carry them all out. Some of these fantasies will never be willingly carried out. There is a big difference between real actions and the libido-induced products of one's imagination.

Writing often plays an important role in sado-masochistic games. One may for instance write a contract to declare one's submission to the master/mistress, as in Venus in Furs by Sacher-Masoch, in which the character Severin signs such a contract with his mistress Wanda. In keeping with this written tradition, a couple can draw up a questionnaire on the practices each has already tried, and on those they have heard about and would like to try. Every wish and desire can be negotiated. Such a document will enable you to define the games you want to play very clearly. It will also be very handy if and when you want to try SM games outside your couple. It will allow you to easily and rapidly evaluate your sexual compatibility with others.

Never inflict real humiliations or injuries on the "dominated" person:

This does not necessarily mean that spankings or "punishments" cannot be included in SM games. But non-consensual or excessive injuries to the body or mind must be ruled out. In domination/submission games, some pain may lead to the experience of a new pleasure, but it is not an end in itself.

Using a safeword: One of the characteristics of SM games is that they may lead you to push your limits further. If you enjoy these games, you will always be wanting to discover new horizons, you will look for ever stronger sensations, you will want to do and feel things you have never experienced before. However, it may happen that you start to feel uncomfortable during a particular game, and it would be useful to be able to stop it with a simple safeword that you have determined beforehand. This safeword would immediately let your partner know that something is not to your liking and you want to get out of the situation NOW. It may not help to cry or ask for mercy as such manifestations could be taken as added erotic stimuli. Do not use passwords like "Stop!" "I can't take it any more!" or "Ouch!": this could result in confusion. Instead, choose a completely unrelated word such as "Athena", "computer" or "Rolling Stone"... And if you are going to be gagged, you should also think of a particular gesture to make. When the safeword or the agreed gesture is said or done, the action must cease immediately. If your partner does not stop, beware: all of your limits are threatened.

2 Master/mistress and slave: the role of each

In an SM game, the master/mistress is not necessarily the man and the slave is not necessarily the woman. One of the two partners plays the dominant role and the other the submissive one, but they depend on each other to satisfy their individual needs. Each partner has different needs, but dom(me) and sub are equal. And many couples often switch roles.

The degree to which the game is played depends on whether the partners are dom(me) and sub or master/mistress and slave: the dependence is stronger between the slave and the master. It is sometimes symbolised by a tattoo, piercing or other physical sign showing the bond of possession between the slave and the master/mistress.

The role of the dom(me) or the master/mistress:

The role of the dom(me) or master/mistress is to control the actions, the emotions and the desires of the sub or the slave. Inexperienced "masters/mistresses" think that domming consists simply of giving orders to their "slaves" in order to satisfy their sexual fantasies. But the role of the master/mistress is much more complex. He or she should be able to arouse the desire to please and satisfy in the slave. The master/mistress is also a protector, a teacher and a lover. As a protector, the master/mistress must appear stronger than the slave and than others. This strength is not necessarily physical, but also a mental, intellectual strength.

As a teacher, the dominant partner must be wise and honest. The teacher should earn the respect of the student and should not arbitrarily punish him or her. The teacher's role is not to inflict pain or humiliation, but to show the way and set goals for the student; to teach the student how to please and how to love. As a lover, the master/mistress should become the slave's principal source of desire. The dom(me) may invent scenes according to his/her own desires, but must also cater to the wishes and desires of the sub.

Vanessa Ryan

The role of the submissive or slave:

The slave deserves to be treated with respect and dignity. He or she may freely express his or her opinion and fully participate in the activities of the master/mistress. The sub learns how to please the master/mistress. The slave knows that good behaviour will be rewarded but that bad behaviour will be punished. But the slave often finds ways to manipulate the master/mistress according to his or her own desires. Many written testimonies show that in the dialectic relationship between "master/mistress and slave", the real dom(me) is not always the one who appears to be. Indeed, the master/mistress exists only thanks to the slave. And when the slave stops playing, the master/mistress no longer exists, and the game ends.

Fetishism

Fetishism only affects men. It can be defined as the compulsive need to see or touch an object or part of the body as a stimulus to sexual arousal. Fetishists venerate such objects or body parts, as they constitute a very powerful means of sexually arousal.

Objet types

Fetish objects most often are suggestive of the female genital organs, such as hair, fur or underclothes, and sometimes feminine accessories like jewels or women's shoes.

Causes

This behaviour, classed as sexual 'deviance' is usually explained by a psychological imbalance. Freud theorised that fetishists are deeply afraid of women who, lacking a penis, provoke in them a castration anxiety. He thought that fetishists, incapable of confronting women directly, use substitute objects to approach them indirectly, thus relieving their fears.

Exhibitionis

An exhibitionist, or an exhibitionist couple, derive sexual pleasure from being discovered and seen by others.

Practice
Exhibitionists seek out opportunities to be naked in public places. They may even indulge their fetish in front of many people. Sometimes this is because they like their bodies and/or their way of making love, believing it to be wonderful and unique, and seeking to show it off. Women who dress in mini-skirts and sexy underwear are practising a less extreme form of exhibitionism. The same is true of couples who indulge in public displays of affection.

Voyeuris

Voyeurism is stereotypically considered a masculine fetish. It consists of spying on people who are naked or indulging in sexual acts, without their realising it.

Practice

The voyeur prefers to avoid the sex act and remain a spectator: the spectacle is enough to produce pleasure. This pleasure can be heightened by the idea that s/he could be discovered and that the victims will feel humiliated by having been watched.

Causes

Freud said this predilection was often due to a repressive and authoritarian upbringing, leading to sexual issues which are repressed during childhood. Freud claims that voyeurs remain at an infantile psychological stage which prevents them from indulging in "normal" sexual activity.

However, we all have a certain natural tendency to voyeurism, which is not necessarily sexual. Most of us find it quite exciting to catch sight of a couple making love through the window of a hotel room!

Vibrators, Dildos and Lubricants

In theory, almost anything can take the role of a "sex toy." Other than two human bodies, anything else introduced into sex play qualifies as either prophylaxis (contraception and disease prevention) or recreation, i.e., a toy. For our purposes, a sex toy is any object brought into sex play to enhance the pleasure of both people involved.

There was some debate as to the question "what is a sex toy?" for the purposes of this FAQ. Some argued that this FAQ should cover those items that are only specifically for sex, whereas others rightly pointed out that that would exclude from discussion some very popular forms of sexual enhancement such as linger or food. A sex toy will be anything that is either specifically intended for sexual enhancement or commonly used for same. There are people out there that find mountain goats, hand puppets, and UN*x System Administration manuals suitable for sexual enhancement, but that's not "common."

THE VIBRATOR

Vibrators come in three distinct 'types'. Many women find satisfaction in this most common (and more often thought of), the classic penis-shaped, battery powered shaft of plastic. These suffer, however, from a lack of real power and inconvenient battery death.

The second type of vibrator, the 'wand' vibrator, overcomes these problems with wall current. These large, club-shaped vibrators provide LOTS of stimulation, and wall current provides all the power you could ask for, but the designers apparently intended for people not to view these things as sex toys, but as "personal massagers," and the ungainliness of these things reflects that.

The third type of vibrator, the 'handle' or 'coil' type, looks vaguely like a small hairdryer with a small, perpendicular shaft out of the thicker end to accommodate a variety of soft plastic or latex heads. The best of all possible worlds, these vibrators never die, fit in one hand, and can provide a variety of sensations.

Shower Massagers make a wonderful variation on the classic vibrator, and if you enjoy the warmth and wetness of the tub, you probably want to consider investing in a shower massager. Like the wand and handle vibrators, shower massagers have a host of uses beyond masturbation, too!

Before using any mechanical vibrator, apply lubrication! Your lover probably does not rank friction burns in the same category as love bites. Use a water-based lubricant, such as K-Y (always recommended), Astroglide, or Wet.

Do not purchase a vibrator specifically designed to deliver heat to the body as a sexual device. If they work on muscles, great, but don't use them on your cunts and cocks. I know of at least one case where a woman burned herself with one of these things because her climaxes were so strong she didn't notice how much the heater had burned her.

No mechanical piece of plastic can replace the love and affection of a human being; try to see the vibrator as just another toy, and not as competition. Vibrators cannot do the dishes or take out the garbage, and they cannot give hugs or kisses.

Some women do experience a temporary 'desensitization'

after the effects of a powerful vibrator but put the toy away for a week and sensitivity returns to normal. There is no clinical evidence that vibrators cause long-term desensitization.

THE DILDO

Dildos come in many different shapes and sizes, but all of them are meant to do one thing: in some way, shape, or form, they are meant to be a substitute or symbol for a real penis. If you are inclined to believe Freud, then the Washington Monument could be considered a dildo. For our purposes, though, a dildo is a sex toy, usually made of latex or silicone, designed to be inserted into some bodily orifice for sexual pleasure.

People use dildos for a variety of purposes. Although most women can orgasm through clitoral stimulation, many do enjoy the feeling of something hard and thrusting inside them during masturbation. Many men, gay or otherwise, feel the same way, using small (or as your tastes go, large) dildos for anal stimulation. A dildo can be used with a harness to give a woman a penis she can thrust with and still keep her hands free.

Buying a dildo involves a number of factors, such as length, thickness, hardness and texture. It is strongly recommended that you comparison shop with your hands, looking for one with a smooth surface made of a firm, but not too firm, latex. Dildo shopping is a very personal activity, and you should take your time buying one.

The two most common materials for a dildo are silicone and latex. Silicone is usually more expensive, but most people who use dildos regularly agree that its qualities of matching body temperature and its general texture make it the superior material. As with anything, you get what you pay for.

The most important thing to remember is that you should start small. Buy dildos you *know* you can probably handle, rather than ones you hope to be able to handle. Get your money's worth out of any toy you buy.

LUBRICANTS

A "lubricant" (sometimes referred to as a "sex lube," or just "lube"), is usually a water-based, condom-friendly liquid or jelly used to enhance or replace a woman's natural lubrication. Some people regard lubricants as a must-have item in this age of safer sex and they are an essential ingredient to successful anal intercourse. The use of a lubricant on the inside of a condom can make the sensations delivered to the penis much stronger.

Prior to the current, safer-sex era, many people used oil-based lubricants, using vaseline, vegetable oil, or mineral oil. None of these are particularly healthy. Oils coat the inside of the vagina and rectum, providing a breeding ground for dangerous bacteria.

Petroleum-based oils destroy latex upon contact, making them useless for use with condoms for safer sex or contraception. Even monogamous couples who don't have to worry about safer sex if they use certain forms of contraception: if an oil destroys the latex of condoms, it will also destroy the latex of diaphragms, cervical caps, and sponges, as well as the protective coatings around some IUDs.

Most lubricants are made up of one or (more commonly) several of the following: glycerin, hydroxyethyl cellulose, or propylene glycol. Some add aloe vera or vitamin E acetate. All add a pH balancing agent, and most have some sort of preservative, since the first three items are all essentially food additives, "thickening agents." Look at a container of Slime in a toy store -- the same three primary ingredients.

"Best lubricant" is a non-sequitor, since lubricant choice is as personal to taste as food. Some people like it thick, others runny, and others need it to be slick enough to grease their engines and others need it to last long enough to go for hours. Small sampler bottles (1 oz.) are available for a dollar a piece -- buy one of each and try them out. Figure out which one you like best.

Safe Oral Sex & Sexually Transmitted Diseases

Like all sexual activity, oral sex carries some risk, particularly when one partner or the other is known to be infected with HIV, when either partner's HIV status is not known, and/or when one or the other partner is not monogamous or injects drugs. Numerous studies have demonstrated that oral sex can result in the transmission of HIV and other sexually transmitted diseases (STDs).

Abstaining from oral, anal, and vaginal sex altogether or having sex only with a mutually monogamous, uninfected partner are the only ways that individuals can be completely protected from the sexual transmission of HIV.

Common Practice

Oral sex involves giving or receiving oral stimulation (i.e. sucking or licking) to the penis, the vagina, and/or the anus. Fellatio is the technical term used to describe oral contact with the penis. Cunnilingus is the technical term which describes oral-vaginal sex.

Anilingus (sometimes called "rimming") refers to oral-anal contact.

Studies indicate that oral sex is commonly practiced by sexually active male-female and same-gender couples of various ages, including adolescents. Although there are only limited national data about how often adolescents engage in oral sex, some data suggest that many adolescents who engage in oral sex do not consider it to be sex; therefore they may use oral sex as an option to experience sex while still, in their minds, remaining abstinent.

Moreover, many consider oral sex to be a safe or no risk sexual practice. In a recent national survey of teens conducted for The Kaiser Family Foundation, 26 percent of sexually active 15- to 17-year-olds surveyed responded that one "cannot become infected with HIV by having unprotected oral sex," and an additional 15 percent didn't know whether or not one could become infected in that manner.

There is Risk

The risk of HIV transmission from an infected partner through oral sex is much smaller than the risk of HIV transmission from anal or vaginal sex. Because of this, measuring the exact risk of HIV transmission as a result of oral sex is very difficult. In addition, since most sexually active individuals practice oral sex in addition to other forms of sex, such as vaginal and/or anal sex, when transmission occurs, it is difficult to determine whether or not it occurred as a result of oral sex or other more risky sexual activities.

Finally, several co-factors can increase the risk of HIV transmission through oral sex, including oral ulcers, bleeding gums, genital sores, and the presence of other STDs.

Scientists have documented HIV infection transmission with oral sex. Although the risk is many times smaller than anal or vaginal sex, HIV has been transmitted to receptive partners through fellatio, even in cases when insertive partners didn't ejaculate. The risk of HIV transmission during cunnilingus and anilingus is extremely low compared to anal or vaginal sex, but a few cases have been linked to this type of sex.

The study results emphasize that any type of sexual activity with an infected person is a risk of HIV transmission. Oral sex with someone who is infected with HIV is certainly not risk free.

Other STDs

Scientists have documented a number of other sexually transmitted diseases that have also been transmitted through oral sex. Herpes, syphilis, gonorrhea, genital warts (HPV), intestinal parasites (amebiasis), and hepatitis A are examples of STDs which can be transmitted during oral sex with an infected partner.

Reduce Your Risk
The consequences of HIV infection are life-long, life-threatening, and extremely serious. For cunnilingus or anilingus, plastic food wrap, a condom cut open, or a dental dam can serve as a physical barrier to prevent transmission of HIV and many other STDs.

Because anal and vaginal sex are much riskier and because most individuals who engage in unprotected oral sex also engage in unprotected anal and/or vaginal sex, the exact proportion of HIV infections attributable of oral sex alone is not known, but is likely to be small. This has led some people to believe that oral sex is completely safe. It is not.

SEXUALLY TRANSMITTED DISEASES
HIV / AIDS (ACQUIRED IMMUMO-DEFICIENCY SYNDROME)

Full name:
Human Immunodeficiency Virus/Acquired Immunodeficiency Syndrome. It is important to distinguish between the two. HIV is the virus that ultimately causes AIDS. AIDS is a syndrome, a collection of symptoms associated with HIV infection.

Symptoms:
People infected with HIV may have no symptoms for up to

fifteen years. During this time, they are capable of infecting anyone they have sex with or donate blood to. Initial symptoms of HIV infection include inexplicable weight loss, persistent fever, swollen lymph nodes, and reddish spots on the skin (Karposi's Sarcoma).

HIV causes the destruction of the immune system. It's most pronounced symptoms, therefore, are opportunistic infections of pneumocystis carinii, fungal infections, tuberculosis, and various herpes forms.

Transmission:

In a person infected with HIV, the virus can be present in the body's semen, blood, and breast milk. It can also be present, in much smaller quantities, in vaginal secretion, saliva, and tears.

The AIDS virus can be transmitted via any of these fluids, but only the first two -- semen and blood -- are likely to be involved. Anal sex is the most commonly perceived method of transfer, but vaginal sex has been repeatedly shown to transmit HIV. Men are less likely than women to be infected through vaginal sex, but there are recorded cases of men having been infected this way. Cunnilingus and fellatio have also been established as capable of transmitting the virus. Sexual activities, not sexual orientation, transmit the virus.

HIV cannot be passed on through casual contact, hugging, hand-shaking, touching the sweat of an infected person, or mosquito bites.

Testing:

The HIV test shows the presence of antibodies to HIV. It does not show the presence of the virus: the body first has to develop antibodies, which normally takes about six weeks. Hence, a positive result means that someone has antibodies and could possibly develop AIDS in the future. A negative result means that someone does not have antibodies *at the moment*. If there is a reason to think that exposure was more recent than six weeks, then a test taken immediately can only serve as a baseline to compare against a test taken later. Within six months of HIV infection, 99% of the population will test positive. No one should be tested for HIV without first obtaining counseling and ensuring *beforehand* support from his or her family or friends.

Treatment:

There is no cure for HIV / AIDS. Right now most scientists agree that if you are infected with HIV, you will eventually die of AIDS. Treatment may fend off infections, however the typical course is for one overwhelming infection to follow another until the victim succumbs. Various drugs may slow the virus, but right now there is no cure.

GONORRHEA, CLAP

Male Symptoms:

Yellowish discharge from the penis. Painful, frequent urination. Symptoms develop from two to thirty days after infection. Roughly 20% of infected men have no symptoms. Later stages of the infection may move into the prostate, seminal vesicles, and epididymis, causing severe pain and fever.
Rare cases can lead to septic arthritis. Untreated, goorrhea can lead to sterility.

Female Symptoms:

Under half of women with gonorrhea show no symptoms, or symptoms so mild they are commonly ignored. Early symptoms include increased vaginal discharge, irritation of the external genitals, pain or burning on urination and abnormal menstrual bleeding. Women who are untreated may develop severe complications. The infection will usually spread to the uterus, Fallopian tubes, and ovaries, causing Pelvic Inflammatory

Disease (PID). PID, though not only caused by gonorrhea, is the most common cause of female infertility. Early symptoms of PID are lower abdominal pain, fever, nausea, vomiting, and pain during intercourse.

Transmission:

The bacteria that causes gonorrhea can be passed through sexual contact, such as intercourse, fellatio, anal sex, cunnilingus and even kissing, although the last is rare.

Treatment:
Gonorrhea is a bacterial infection, and is therefore treated with standard antibiotics, usually a member of the penicillin family. Tetracycline drugs frequently do not cure gonorrhea, especially in cases of anal infection. One variety of gonorrhea, penicilliase-producing N. gonorrhea, is immune to penicillin, and drugs of the cyclosporin family may be necessary.

SYPHILIS

Symptoms:

Primary Stage:

A chancre sore develops at the site of infection from two to four weeks after infection has occurred. The chancre is painless 75% of the time. The chancre starts as a dull red spot, turns into a pimple, which ulcerates, forming a round or oval sore with a red rim. The sore heals in 4-6 weeks - however, the infection is still present. The chancre is usually found on the genitals or anus, but can appear on any part of the skin.

Secondary Stage:
One week to six months after the chancre heals. Pale red or pinkish rash appears (often on palms or soles) fever, sore throat, headaches, joint pains, poor appetite, weight loss, hair loss. Moist sores may appear around the genitals or anus and

are highly infectious. Symptoms usually last three to six months, but can come and go.
Latent Stage:

No apparent symptoms and the carrier is no longer contagious. However, the organism is insinuating itself into the host's tissues. 50 to 70 percent of carriers pass the rest of their lives without the disease leaving this stage. The reminder passes into Last Stage syphilis.

Last Stage:
Serious heart problems, eye problems, brain and spinal cord damage, with a high probability of paralysis, insanity, blindness or death.

Transmission:
Nominally sexual contact, but can be transmitted by blood transfusion or from an infected pregnant woman to her fetus.

Treatment:
Penicillin by injection, or a two-week regimen of tetracycline, is the standard treatment for syphilis. Two follow-up blood tests two weeks apart after ending treatment are necessary to ensure the treatment is complete.
The first three stages of syphilis are completely curable, and even in the last stage syphilis can be stopped. With the present medical technology to diagnose and treat syphilis, no one should ever suffer the effects of last-stage syphilis.

GENTIAL WARTS AND HUMAN PAPILLOMA VIRUS (HPV)

Full name:
Human Papilloma Virus

Symptoms:
Half of the people infected with HPV do not show any symptoms. When symptoms are present, they are small, visible

warts (papillomas) appearing at the tip of the penis or at the opening of vagina. In women, HPV also causes cervical lesions. Warts can occur anywhere on the shaft of penis or the scrotum in men, and anywhere around the labial area or inside the vagina in women. In women, an abnormal Pap smear may indicate cervical lesions, but a coloscopy is necessary to confirm this.

Transmission:
The virus is transmitted through sexual contact. Warts are considered very contagious even in people who show no visible symptoms.

Treatment:
Warts are pinpoint infections, and can be treated as such. Podophyllin solution, trichlorocetic acid, and fluorouracil cream are three chemical solutions used to burn warts from the skin. Liquid nitrogen or lasers are sometimes used, as well as electrodessication. A six-month check-up is necessary to confirm that all the warts were destroyed, and even then a small percentage of people may experience a recurrence of warts within 18 months.

GENITAL HERPES, HERPES SIMPLEX VIRUS (HSV)

Full Name:
Herpes Simplex Virus I and Herpes Simplex Virus II. HSV-I is most often associated with cold sores or fever blisters about the mouth and lips, while HSV-II is associated with sores around the genital area. There is some crossover, however, and each virus will survive quite comfortably in both regions.

Symptoms:
Herpes is marked by clusters of small, painful blisters on the genitals. After a few days, the blisters burst, leaving small ulcers. In men, the blisters usually appear on the penis, but can appear in the urethra or rectum. In women, they usually appear on the labia, but can appear on the cervix and anal area. First outbreaks are accompanied by fever, headache, and muscle

soreness for two or more consecutive days in 39% of men and 68% of women. Other relatively common symptoms include painful urination discharge from the urethra or vagina, and tender, swollen lymph nodes in the groin. These symptoms tend to disappear within two weeks. Aseptic meningitis occurs in 8 percent of cases, eye infections in 1% of cases, and infection of the cervix in 88% of infected women. Skin lesions last on average 16.5 days in men, 19.7 in women. Secondary symptoms are most prominent in the first four days and then gradually diminish.

Recurrence:
 None in 10% of cases. Frequency for the remaining population is from once a month to once every few years. The majority of sufferers do not have repeat attacks after a few years. Most repeat attacks are less severe than the initial attack.

Transmission:
 Generally by sexual contact. Direct contact with infected genitals can cause transmission via intercourse, rubbing genitals together, oral genital contact, anal sex, or oral/anal contact. In addition, normally protected areas of skin can become infected if there is a cut, rash, sore. Herpes viruses can be spread in some instances by kissing, if one participant has the infection sited in or near the mouth.

Treatment:
 There is no medical cure for herpes. Treatment with acyclovir reduces pain and viral reproduction during outbreaks of sores, although it will not delay or prevent recurrences.

CRABS, PUBIC LICE

Full name:
 Phthirus pubis, the pubic louse or crab louse.

Symptoms:
Pubic lice are tiny insects that infest pubic hair. They somewhat resemble tiny crabs, hence their common name. The most common symptom is intense itching, usually felt mostly at night. Some victims have no symptoms, others may develop an allergic rash.

Transmission:
Nominally through sexual contact, however they may be picked up through use of sheets, towels or clothing used by an infected person.

Treatment:
Various shampoos and lotions exist to kill lice; another solution is simply to shave off the pubic hair and shower vigorously afterwards. All bedding should also be disinfected.

NONSPECIFIC URETHRITIS (NSU) OR NONGONOCCAL URETHRITIS (NGU)

Caused by:

Chlamydia trachomatous, T. mycoplasma, Ureaplasma urealyticum, Mycolasma hominis. An estimated one-quarter of cases are not caused by infectious agents, but are allergic reactions to latex or spermicide.

Symptoms:
Similar to gonorrhea but usually milder. Urethral discharge is generally thin and clear. Planned Parenthood estimates that half of the women with one of these diseases don't know it. NSU/NGU in women can lead to pelvic inflammatory disease (PID) and sterility.
Transmission:
In cases involving a pathogen, sexual intercourse, as well as hands with semen or vaginal secretions on them infecting the eye.

Treatment:
Penicillin is generally not effective against NGU/NSU-causing organisms. Tetracycilne is generally prescribed; sulfa drugs are effective against chlamydia but not the others.

HEPATITIS B, SERUM HEPATITIS

Caused by:
Hepatitis B Virus (HBV)

Symptoms:

About half of those who get hepatitis B will suffer from an inflammation of the liver, called acute hepatitis. Many people with hepatitis B mistake the symptoms for other illnesses, such as the flu, while others are more seriously affected and may miss school or work for months. Other common symptoms include skin rashes and arthritis, nausea, vomiting, loss of appetite, malaise, abdominal pain, and jaundice (yellowing of the eyes and skin).

Transmission:

Hepatitis B is transmitted through contact with the bodily fluids of an infected person, and that includes sexual contact. It is a considered a highly infectious disease and should be taken seriously.

Treatment:
There is no cure for hepatitis B. There is a vaccine, however, that is very effective. It is also expensive. Consult your physician. A small percentage of people who acquire hepatitis B will carry the virus in their bloodstreams for the rest of their lives as carriers.

TRICHOMONIASIS, TRICH, TRICK

Caused by:
Trichomonas vaginalis, a flagellated protozoan.

Symptoms:
Similar to gonorrhea but usually milder. Symptoms in women include itching, burning, vaginal or vulval redness, unusual vaginal discharge, frequent and/or painful urination, and discomfort during intercourse, and, in severe cases, abdominal pain.
Symptoms in men include unusual penile discharge, painful urination, and uncanny tingling sensation inside the penis.

Transmission:
Trichomoniasis is transmitted by penis-in-vagina intercourse or vulva-to-vulva contact with an infected partner. Women can contract the disease from infected men or women, but men usually get it only from infected women. The protozoan can survive for a time on sheets and towels, and an infection can possibly be transmitted by sharing those objects.

Treatment:
The antibiotic metronidazole is generally used to treat trichomonas infection.

Printed in the United Kingdom
by Lightning Source UK Ltd.
129610UK00003B/320/A